Poor Man's Guide to Bottle Collecting

Poor Man's Guide to Bottle Collecting

BY
FEROL AUSTEN

GARDEN CITY, NEW YORK

DOUBLEDAY & COMPANY, INC.

1971

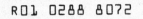
Library of Congress Catalog Card Number 74–150877
Copyright © 1971 by New Hampshire Publishing Co.

Printed in the United States of America

Preface

This book is written for the incipient bottle collector who has yet to pull on a pair of strong hiking boots and trudge along a country lane in search of buried treasure.

More specifically it addresses itself to the collector who has dug up a few good items already, cleaned and polished them to jewel-like brilliance, displayed them on a shelf to be admired by friends and captive relatives, and is now ready to go on to bigger things.

It is hoped that this book will perk an interest in the story behind the bottles and help weave the various periods of bottlemaking into a comprehensive chronological design.

It is not enough to know something of only the bottles in one's own collection. The collector must know how his bottles fit into the total bottle picture.

No attempt has been made here to produce a monumental work—or, for that matter, a definitive one. What the writer has attempted to do is to provide thumbnail sketches of the various categories and kinds of bottles, the times in which they were made and used, and how they relate to still other categories of bottles.

Antique bottles and bottle collecting are huge subjects. However, there have emerged several experts in the field, and the collector is fortunate that so much fine material is at hand.

In the preparation of this book the writer utilized innumerable sources. She is especially grateful for the following:

Bottle Collecting in New England by John P. Adams. Somersworth, New Hampshire: New Hampshire Publishing Co. 1969.

Old Time Bottles Found in the Ghost Towns by Lynn Blumenstein. Salem, Oregon: Old Time Bottle Publishing Co. 1966.

Grand Old American Bottles by Dr. Larry Freeman. Watkins Glen, New York: Century House. 1964.

The Story of American Historical Flasks by Helen McKearin. The Corning Museum of Glass, Corning Glass Center, Corning, N.Y. Summer 1953.

Two Hundred Years of American Blown Glass by Helen and George S. McKearin. Garden City, New York: Doubleday & Co., Inc. 1950.

American Glass by Mary Harrod Northend. New York: Tudor Publishing Co. 1926. Reprinted 1947.

Collectors' Guide to Antique American Glass by Marvin D. Schwartz. Garden City, New York: Doubleday & Co., Inc. 1969.

A Guide for Insulator Collectors by John C. Tibbitts. Sacramento, California: The Little Glass Shack. 1967.

Bitters Bottles by Richard Watson. New York and Toronto: Thomas Nelson & Sons Ltd. 1965.

PREFACE

For their invaluable assistance in obtaining photographs with which to properly illustrate the text, the author wishes to express appreciation to Mr. Kenneth M. Wilson, assistant director and curator of the Corning Museum of Glass, and Miss Jane Shadel, research assistant at Corning; Mr. John W. Keefe, assistant curator of the Toledo Museum of Art; and Miss Catherine Fennelly, who made available the photo files at Old Sturbridge Village.

Thanks also go to Miss Christa König, who photographed Miss Jane Shadel, research assistant at Corning; Mr. John Ballentine of the New Hampshire Publishing Company, for his patience, enthusiastic assistance, and constant encouragement.

F.A.

Contents

CHAPTER I

An Introduction to Bottle Collecting

Collecting bottles is just like collecting anything else. After you've unearthed your first old bottle from a pile of debris, cleaned it, polished it, held it to the light, and seen it as a shimmering thing of beauty, you'll be "hooked."

This is because every bottle you dig out of the earth will become a piece of your life, just as it was a silent witness of countless other lives. If you're lucky, its history will go back much further than your own.

Old bottles of the right kind are worth money too.

But whether a bottle that you have lovingly burnished back to existence is worth fifty cents or five hundred dollars on the open market, or whether it turns out to be a priceless museum piece, you'll find yourself having a lot of fun.

The same thing that spurred the gold seekers of 1849 takes hold of the bottle hunter. Every new find only whets his appetite for more.

Our forays into the woods have sometimes lasted for days, even whole vacations. Other people go on camping trips. So do we; only ours turn out to be combination camping and bottle-hunting trips. It's amazing what you find when your eye is attuned to the right frequency. Even our German shepherd is becoming adept in sniffing out likely candidates for our small museum.

That's another good thing about bottle collecting. It can be a whole-family activity, unless, of course, you prefer to explore on your own.

Like many collectors, we are not terribly discriminate. Except for the commonest sort of modern everyday bottle—the kind you see by the hundreds along the highway and in city dumps—we find it difficult to pass up anything. Even if they aren't "worth" anything, most glass bottles of any vintage are, when properly cleaned and displayed, rather beautiful.

We've heard of people who have built houses out of bottles, but we haven't quite come to that. When the bottles begin to pile up, we give them away to new collectors.

Another reason to be careful in passing up bottles is that it is difficult to identify a very dirty bottle, and the oldest and most valuable types will in most cases be encrusted with layers (and years) of soil and other impurities. It would be easy to discard a really valuable specimen.

But why do people collect bottles? Why not stamps or dolls or rocks instead? What's so great about spending weekends trudging through woods and swamps and inhaling the lingering—and often far from pleasant—fumes of city dumping stations?

Every hobby has its own particular following, and each in its own way tells us something of history or life as it once was. From our various collections, whether they be postage stamps or matchbook covers—if we have been serious in studying them as well as simply amassing them—we learn something about other people, other periods in time, other ways of life.

Bottles have a unique story to tell. In fact, it is possible through bottles alone to trace a comprehensive history of nations and civilizations. The entire history of a young country such as the United States, from the first settlement in Jamestown in 1607, right through to the present day, can be traced through the bottles that have been an important part of everyday life from that time to this.

Actually, glassmaking was the first industry in the New World. The first crude products made by the glasshouse in Capt. John Smith's colony at Jamestown, Virginia, were followed by the more elegant wares that were made later in glasshouses in Pennsylvania. The huge, round-bellied bottles filled with whiskey that were provided the American colonies by the English were supplanted by the demijohns and carboys made by the independent Americans after the Revolution.

Hard-drinking frontiersmen, hewing homes out of the wilderness, brought a great demand for pocket flasks so that they could carry refreshments with them. As men pushed west in the search of land and later for gold, and as more homesteads were established across the new country, the demand for bottles of all kinds grew and grew.

America entered on a bottle "binge." There were whiskey flasks and bottles for every purpose, and they commemorated historical events, landmarks of achievement, the opening of the West, the railroad, and the crossing of the Rocky Mountains. There were bottles glorifying United States Presidents, presidential candidates, and other celebrities.

Competitor bottlemakers and distillers vied with each other in bringing out new and novel designs to satisfy the demands from what had become a bottle-happy public.

If we are really to enjoy this hobby of ours to the full, it is necessary for us, as we go about unearthing some of these relics of the past, to know something about where they fit in the long line of history.

You won't always be digging in the local dump or in a neighbor's back yard. As your interest in bottles grows (and this is where the interest *should* lie, and not merely in collecting alone), you will spread your wings and perhaps find yourself digging in parts of the country where bottles of an entirely different era can be found.

If you come upon, say, some rare pre-Revolutionary War bottle, how will you know it, unless bottles as witnesses of the past have become a meaningful phase of your bottle collecting?

Rare bottles have been found in Indian graves in Rhode Island, in outhouses in western ghost towns, and in New England cellar holes. The trail of old bottles leads us all over the United States, and the collector must be alert for the telltale signs of a hidden cache.

Of course, people were a little neater decades ago than they seem to be today. Until the invention of the bottlemaking machine in 1903, consumers tended to save their bottles. Perhaps it was a carry-over from frugal ways. When they did finally discard bottles, they usually buried them in neat piles, along with the garbage and other trash.

So that this business of collecting bottles will become more fascinating, more impelling, more satisfying to us, let's take a look at some of the exciting stories of glassmaking and bottlemaking: how bottles came to occupy such an important place in everyday American life, and how we can recognize a good find when we come upon it.

CHAPTER II

The First Glassmakers

Since 1500 B.C. men have been making glass bottles, and each bottle has its own significance as a link in a long chain of human history and behavior.

No one really knows when the first glass was made. It was most likely an accident, whenever it happened. One of the favorite tales is that of the Phoenician sailors who were caught in a storm one night on their way back to Syria from Egypt and blown ashore.

They were carrying a cargo of natron, or soda, and when the hungry group made their supper that night on the bleak shore, they used some of the slabs of natron to rest their cooking pots on. A fire was made from materials at hand, and in the morning the surprised sailors awoke to see that some of the natron had melted and fused with sand and ashes from the seaweed, and thus glass was born.

It's a romantic, much-loved story, but it is unlikely that a simple beach fire could have reached the required intensity for making glass, some 1800 degrees Fahrenheit.

It is much more likely that glassmaking was slowly evolved from a series of happy accidents from which someone finally deduced that certain ingredients heated to a certain temperature produced a pleasing and useful substance.

We know from relics recovered from ancient tombs that glass was made in Egypt and also created with artistic refinement. Among a variety of glass trinkets were found beads and necklaces and small objects made in the forms of popular deities. They also made small decorated bottles and small medallion-type discs that were probably used for coins.

Eventually traders brought samples of glasswork to all parts of the Mediterranean. At that time wooden and clay vessels were used to store liquids and often leaked their valuable stores. One can imagine the delight of merchants as they eagerly vied to purchase glass containers to hold their fine oils and wines.

Although for about 1200 years small glass bottles were made by using a solid metal rod with which to dip and redip the glass in a molten mass, the blowpipe was not invented until around 300 B.C. It seems incredible that it should have taken so long for someone to get the idea to substitute a hollow rod for a solid one and to blow through it to produce a workable, hollow ball of glass.

The Phoenicians are generally given credit for this remarkable invention, and its discovery blew the lid off of glassmaking. The whole Mediterranean became involved. The Romans took up the art in earnest, and by 200 B.C. they had made themselves leaders in the field, as they did in most every other field they tackled. The art spread quickly to other civilized countries; there were glass blowers in Italy, Syria, Greece.

Their skill also increased. By then they had also learned to blow glass into a mold.

Rome held on to her leadership in glassmaking until the fifth century, when this First Golden Age of Glass was abruptly ended by the invasion of Western Europe by the Barbarians. During the Dark Ages that followed, glassmaking flourished in the East, with Constantinople becoming its new center.

At the end of the eleventh century glassmaking had reached Venice, and by the fifteenth century her glass blowers were ready to embark upon the Second Golden Age of Glass, 1250–1650.

Glassmaking was very slow in getting to England. Not until 1557 did she start turning out wares. However, when the new industry finally blossomed, it bloomed spectacularly, and England gave a new kind of glass to the world: "flint" glass. The addition of lead to the glass mixture gave this new glass a brilliancy that was lacking in the other glass of the day. And as it was also softer, it was easier to cut and engrave.

By the time glassmaking came to the New World, it was already a refined art.

CHAPTER III

Glassmaking in the American Colonies

The settlers in Jamestown, Virginia, however, were less concerned with glass as a cultural refinement than they were with it as a necessity for life in the wilderness.

For one thing, they needed window glass. Green logs were often used to hastily put together cabins, and when this timber dried out, it left large gaping chinks and holes in the walls. Irate housewives and shivering children kept family providers busy trying to keep drafts to a minimum.

Because the transporting of glass overseas was such a problem, glassmakers in England saw more sense in helping the colony at Jamestown make its own.

There was a lot to be said for starting a glassworks in Jamestown. The sand found in Virginia was of the type needed, and there was plenty of wood to provide fuel for the furnaces.

So in the spring of 1608 the London Company sent to Jamestown a small group of skilled workmen, and a glasshouse was set up in the woods about a half mile from the town.

Thus was established, although on an extremely shaky foundation, the first industry in America. It didn't last very long. Quarrels with the Indians, treachery in Capt. John Smith's own ranks, and the inability of the industry to sustain itself ended in failure.

In 1621 another attempt also proved to be short-lived; Indian raids, sickness, and a series of misfortunes brought the venture to an end in 1625. Glassmaking was a tricky enough business. Indian massacres and visits by plague were too much.

For the few years it was in existence, however, the Jamestown glassworks served a purpose. Intrigued by the glistening colored glass beads and necklaces turned out by these craftsmen, friendly Indians often came long distances to trade valuable animal skins and other commodities much needed by the settlers.

There is also evidence that the Jamestown plant turned out table glass and bottles, which were actually taken to England and sold there.

After the failure of the second Jamestown plant in 1625, there was little glassmaking in the American colonies, and the people were almost wholly dependent again on imports from the mother country to fill their needs.

The manufacture of glass in those times was a risky undertaking, fraught with hardships and misadventure. Transportation over rough country roads in springless wagons could only result in a tremendous amount of breakage. Skilled workers were difficult to find and even more difficult to keep. Glassmakers stole workers from each other. The furnaces gobbled up forests so quickly that fuel supplies became a problem. Sometimes the sand wasn't right.

Finally, in 1739, a successful button manufacturer, Caspar Wistar, established what is regarded as the first really successful glasshouse in America. From Rotterdam, Wistar imported glassmakers. His contract with them provided they would teach glassmaking to him and his son, Richard, and to nobody else.

The agreement was a fair one. For this exclusive teaching and glassmaking, Wistar promised the workers one-third of the profits from the business, along with all their expenses in moving and getting settled in the New World. Buoyed by his successful relations with these workers and their families, he later imported other artisans from the Low Countries.

Called Wistarberg, the factory was located on 2000 acres of wooded land near the village of Allowaystown in Salem County in southern New Jersey.

As a result of Wistar's good planning, his glassworks prospered. Products included a wide variety of glassware which included, according to an advertisement in the Pennsylvania *Gazette* of 1769, "Most sort of bottles, gallon, ½ gallon, quart, full measure ½ gallon cafe bottles, snuff and mustard bottles."

Although little remains from Wistarberg that can be identified, we can be sure that these bottles were distinctive and individual. Wistar has not only been credited with having established the first successful flint-glass house in America; his products were known for excellency of design and beauty of color. Study of glass fragments found on the grounds of the Wistarberg factory have shown us that.

Since authenticity is lacking, most collectors refer to glass of this period as South Jersey, or more generally, Early American.

For some forty years Wistar's remarkable factory produced high-quality glassware.

Other glasshouses were busy from time to time. One in Massachusetts, for example, earned a living by supplying bottles for cider that was shipped to the West Indies. But, on the whole, glassmaking was a fitful business and generally lacking in entrepreneurs of any real stature.

One of these was Henry William Stiegel, a German emigrant, who arrived in Philadelphia in 1750. This enterprising young man soon married the daughter of a successful owner of an iron furnace and became a partner in the business. From ironmonger to master glassmaker was a transition made possible only by Stiegel's singular ambition and industry.

After a trip to Bristol, England, which at that time was considered one of the leading glass centers, the young Stiegel brought back with him several German glassworkers and a few English workers as well.

Stiegel had a showman's touch; he didn't do anything in small measure. He established a whole town for his glassmaking enterprise in Pennsylvania which he called Manheim, and in 1763 his factory was producing glass objects of exceptional taste and refinement.

Spurred on by unqualified success, Stiegel built another factory—he was already being called "Baron"—and for nine years Stiegel provided fine bottles and other glassware known for their artistic design and uniformity of form and color. It was, in fact, the first glassware manufactured in the American colonies that was comparable with the best being made in Europe.

Finally, however, the Baron's flamboyant mode of living caught up with him, and he went first into bankruptcy and then into debtor's prison. It was the bitter end of an exciting venture. In fact, poor Stiegel ended up working for a time as a foreman in one of his own factories.

With the exception of window glass, which was always in great demand, there was little glass manufacture in America until the late eighteenth century.

This was the state of glassmaking in the American colonies prior to the Revolution.

As noted before, to collect bottles without at least a general knowledge of their origin and their relation to the times in which they were made and used, is comparable to a stamp collector haphazardly amassing great quantities of perforated bits of blank paper without regard to their place of origin or use. If we have some inkling of where our bottles have been, what purpose they have served, what part they played in the everyday life of another century, we will find our collections greatly enhanced, and our enthusiasm for hunting quickened.

Because the various types of bottles fall into such convenient chronological groups and relate so directly to periods of American history, the writer has chosen to trace the links in the chain of bottle lore by separating them into four main categories: *spirits, medicinal, household,* and *personal.*

A similar method was used by Dr. Larry Freeman in his book, *Grand Old American Bottles.* The author has preferred, however, to include figural bottles in the spirits category and to give personal bottles a section of their own.

2   A *free-blown, globular-shaped carboy, American. Nine-
teen century; Ht: 17¼".*
COURTESY: The Corning Museum of Glass

CHAPTER IV

Spirits Bottles

―――――――

In this group belong many of the so-called glamour specimens of the bottle world.

After the Wistar and Stiegel factories had ceased operations, there was practically no glassmaking, other than the manufacture of widowpanes, in the American colonies.

Those glassmaking enterprises that did spring up now and then were unimportant and short-lived.

England, for her part, did nothing to encourage independent local industry in her colonies; in fact, in her efforts to keep them entirely dependent on the mother country, she went out of her way to discourage any kind of self-maintaining activity at all. Her intention to supply all needs included even glass bottles.

So England shipped great quantities of whiskey and gin to her captive American market. The contents were carried in crude, round-bellied, high-necked Hogarth bottles, demijohns, and wicker-covered carboys.

The black-glass Hogarths, which were about eleven inches tall, were so named because prints of Hogarth's "Rake's Progress" show a similarly shaped bottle. The glass, though very dark, was actually green.

Largest of these early containers was the carboy which could hold up to ten gallons. These huge bottles were often

wicker-covered in an effort to keep breakage on the long voyage across the ocean to a minimum. The demijohns were smaller, and held about four gallons. These free-blown bottles were globular in shape.

Colonial tavernkeepers would empty the contents from these bottles into smaller bottles or decanters, and these would be used to pour the liquor into the waiting glasses of thirsty patrons. There were no "packaged" goods in those days.

England was quite prolific when it came to manufacturing containers for her export trade, and her favorite export customer must certainly have been her American cousins in the New World, who didn't really have much choice in the matter.

England was also intent on keeping glassworkers or formulas for glassmaking from leaving the country. Punishment was severe and swiftly meted out to the glass blower who had notions of bringing his family—and trade—to the New World.

There wasn't anything complicated about the forming of the Hogarths and other heavy black-glass bottles. A blow-pipe formed a large bubble which was then "thrown" so as to stretch the neck. The bottles of this period found in museums and private collections are very often extremely crook-necked and crudely formed.

3 Bottle exported from England to the colonies before the beginning of glassmaking in America. 1700.
COURTESY: Old Sturbridge Village

Impurities, such as iron, in the natural soda, lime, and silica mixture, caused the green coloring in glass. This coloring ranged from very dark to olive amber, and most of the bottles of this early period were made from this mixture. In contrast to the heavy Hogarth-type bottles, which were quite dark, many of the demijohns were light green and often have a misleading fragile appearance.

Even in the early seventeenth century, however, consumers recognized that glass bottles had an esthetic side, as well as a merely functional use. Consequently, the shapes of even ordinary spirits bottles were changed every few years to please a public which had begun to want something better than animal bladders and leaky leather bottles in which to carry their resuscitating liquors.

One field of bottle collecting that is just about closed off for the average collector—except for an extraordinary discovery that crops up now and then and makes news wherever it does—is that of the "seal" bottle.

Most of these extremely rare types are in museums. A few are in large private collections.

These seal bottles, or punts—they are even called "blobs" —are sometimes difficult to identify as to age. For the most part these free-blown bottles are squat and globular, with extremely long necks. They were "sealed" on the shoulder by a circular "lozenge" or blob of hot glass in which was pressed either the name of the owner whose liquor it would hold or the year in which it was made.

5   *Seal, with the initials "I.B.," on the shoulder of a greenish glass wine bottle of English origin. 1750–80; Ht: 27.2 cm.* COURTESY: The Corning Museum of Glass

One of these bottles belonging to Jonathan Swift, the author of *Gulliver's Travels,* has been found in England.

These were very personal bottles, kept for the exclusive use of the individual for whom they were made, and usually stored in his private cellar.

The master, in the elegance of his surroundings, would send the servant below to the private stock to fetch a bottle of whiskey or wine with which to slake the thirsts of his guests. After the contents were consumed, the bottles would be refilled at the local tavern or distillery.

These bottles were small, usually holding about a pint, and were made of the same dark green or "black" glass which characterized the larger Hogarths.

Some are quite old. The seal on one bottle discovered in England in 1933 shows a date of 1690.

A few seal bottles were American-made and generally followed the shape of English seal bottles. Some of these bottles were actually made as late as the early nineteenth century.

After the Revolutionary War, and with England no longer supplying the needs of the Americans, there was a sharp increase in the manufacture of window glass and other glass products. And since there had been no decrease in the demand for whiskey and gin and other strong liquors, bottle manufacturers began to spring up in great numbers.

Their products included a variety of sizes and shapes to suit the variety of uses. There were huge carboys for storing applejack and vinegar. There was a steady demand for decanters, too, and serving bottles of all kinds.

Because sizes and colors vary so much, it is very difficult to identify these early bottles as to exact dates. Since bottlemaking was not yet refined, the earliest types can be determined by the roughness and irregularities in the forms that prevailed at the time. The mouth of the newly formed, still-hot bottle was not collared or rimmed, but simply cut off with shears, leaving a rough edge.

Pontil marks on the bottom of the container are generally another sign of a bottle's age. The pontil mark is the rough, often sharp, point left by the pontil bar. This bar, its end dipped in hot glass, was used to hold the bottom of the glass object when it was detached from the blowpipe. In early years the rod was simply broken off, leaving a pontil scar or mark.

Eventually consumers wanted their own bottles. Aside from the seal bottles, owned by affluent persons, the only bottles owned by individuals for their personal use were those made by glass blowers who at the end of the working day were allowed to use the leftover "gather" to form bottles for themselves. These they either filled with spirits at the local tavern or sold to eager buyers.

6 *This seal, also applied to the shoulder, is a blob of hot glass with the name of the owner or the year of the contents impressed upon it. English.* 1777; *Ht:* 9⅜".
COURTESY: The Corning Museum of Glass

In great demand were pocket bottles that the traveler could carry with him on the hot dusty rides on horseback or in a stifling coach. Crude but handy bottles, usually wearing jackets of leather or other protective material, provided canteen-type refreshment on tiring journeys.

After the Revolutionary War the Pitkin Glassworks was established at East Hartford, Connecticut. Later the factory was moved a few miles to Manchester. Here were manufactured a wide variety of small globular bottles in olive amber, amber, and olive green. They had a double-thick body and were pattern-molded (*see* Glossary of Terms).

These so-called Pitkins, holding about a pint, were also made at many other eastern glasshouses, such as the one in Coventry, Connecticut, which wasn't far from Manchester, and in Keene, New Hampshire.

The Pitkin works, which began producing glass around 1780, took over just about when the Wistarberg factory closed. It is also more than possible that the first glass flasks were made by Wistar and not by Pitkin, although "Pitkin" has since become the generic term for this type of bottle.

Of course, in those days, there was no such thing as a "standard" quart or pint-size bottle. One had to rely pretty much on the skill of the glass blower to approximate sizes to the nearest given measure.

Because of their smallish round shapes, these flasks also became known as "chestnuts," or Pitkin chestnuts. After these bottles were taken from the mold, from which resulted a ribbed design, they were often turned to swirl the ribbing, or simply blown into, in order to "expand" the pattern.

The latter method was often used to "soften" a pattern, such as the popular diamond-quilted patterns. In fact, Stiegel manufactured many of these expanded-mold chestnuts, and the diamond patterns are often referred to as Stiegel types, especially those in the colors of blue and amethyst. However, these could have been the work of a number of glass factories operating at the time.

The bottle collector will be coming across these terms constantly and should familiarize himself with them.

Many of these early chestnut types were highly ornamented with molten glass applied to the outside of the bottles in a variety of swirls and scroggle designs.

This was accomplished in several ways. Sometimes blobs of hot glass were applied to the shoulders of the bottles; this was certainly true of the "seal" bottles, where an imprint was made into the lozenge before it hardened.

Sometimes the technique involved dipping and molding designs by hand. Threads or ribbons of still-plastic glass were also applied to the bottles in various crinkle and looping designs. Crosshatching, swirling, and even the addition

of glass in different colors also gave individual characteristics to bottles, and because of the handwork involved, no two bottles of this period are exactly alike.

The collector should be alert to the fact that many reproductions of these bottles have been made. These include bottles in "sunburst" and Masonic designs, as well as the historicals and marked whiskeys, which we will come to later on.

These early sunburst and Masonic whiskey flasks attained great popularity in the early 1800s. The Masons were an influential and significant part of American life and, until around 1830, Masonic emblems appeared not only on bottles, but on other objects as well. The Masonic flasks were made in pint and half-pint sizes.

The sunburst was one of the first bottle designs. These bottles appeared around 1815 and were made in glasshouses in New York, Connecticut, and New Hampshire. A wide variety of other relief designs was also manufactured, including shell, banjo, and violin forms in several colors.

From about 1820 to 1870, decorated whiskey bottles in hundreds of symbols, themes, and designs were tremendously popular, and competition was fierce among glassmakers to come up with products that would appeal to the public.

9 *Sunburst design on a light green pint flask from Marlboro Street Glass Works, Keene, New Hampshire. 1815–17.* COURTESY: The Corning Museum of Glass

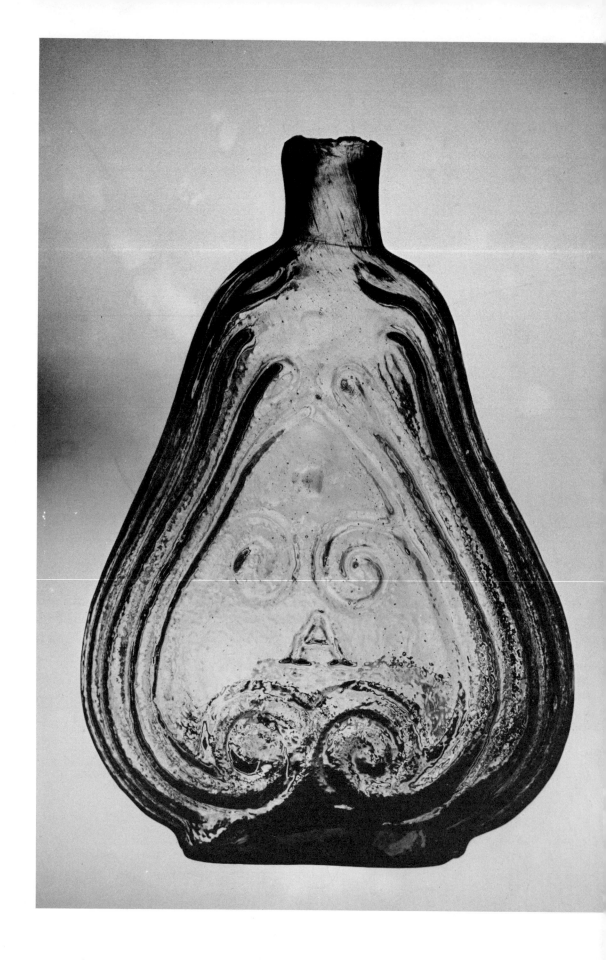

10 *Aquamarine pint flask with the violin-scroll design, of American origin. 1850.*
COURTESY: The Corning Museum of Glass

Among the most popular of the patriotic motifs was the American Eagle. It appeared in over a hundred different forms. In the 1860s these Eagle flasks were made by the New London Glass Works in Connecticut. Other patriotic symbols included the Flag, and the Goddess of Liberty. Columbia was surrounded by stars. The cornucopia, symbol of plenty, also appeared as a patriotic motif on many flasks.

In striving to find designs that would sell, bottlemakers from New England to Indiana to Kentucky snatched at any kind of design that would commemorate an event, memorialize a person, or glorify a celebrity.

Here, in these historical flasks, the collector will find a fascinating segment of bottle lore.

Not only did designs run to sunbursts, fraternal emblems, and general patriotic motifs; a whole new market opened up for bottlemakers to bombard a proud nation with Americana-plus. In a blaze of patriotic fervor, there appeared bottle designs commemorating presidential candidates, political campaign slogans, national events of importance, portraits of celebrities, and everything American but mother and apple pie.

Eulogized in glass, for instance, was the first successful crossing of the Rocky Mountains, the steam locomotive, and the gold rush to Pike's Peak in 1858.

43

George Washington, whose portrait appears on at least sixty different flasks, leads the array of Presidents and presidential candidates. Here we also find Benjamin Franklin, John Adams, Thomas Jefferson, Zachary Taylor, Andrew Jackson, Henry Clay, William Henry Harrison, and John Quincy Adams.

Other celebrities of the day often found their own images staring back at them from some whiskey bottle. The much-sought-after Jenny Lind bottles commemorated the Swedish nightingale's first personal appearance in America.

Other notables "immortalized" in bottles included Lafayette, De Witt Clinton, and Lajos Kossuth, the Hungarian revolutionary hero.

Some of the most interesting bottles to the collector are the marked whiskeys. These were produced in a variety of shapes and sizes and had the name of the contents, such as rye, scotch, etc., stamped in the bottle.

One of the most famous bottles was the so-called "Booz" bottle, in the form of a log cabin. Used to further the "Log Cabin" political campaign of William Henry Harrison, it was made for a Philadelphia distiller by the name of E. G. Booz. It was a fairly large bottle, eight inches high, and it symbolized the birthplace of Harrison, whose aim was to impress voters with his rise from humble circumstances.

11 *Slightly grayish flask, decorated with copper-wheel engravings of foliage, Masonic symbols, and "F. STENGER 1792." Made at the New Bremen, Maryland, Glassmanufactory of John Frederick Amerlung. American; 1792.*
COURTESY: The Corning Museum of Glass

14   A *picture of George Washington and the inscription* "THE FATHER OF HIS COUNTRY" *on green glass pint flask, probably from Dyottville glassworks. American; 1847–48.*
COURTESY: The Corning Museum of Glass

15 *Deep blue pint flask from Kensington Glass Works of Timothy Dyott of Philadelphia. Obverse shows George Washington; reverse shows an Eagle and "T.W.D."; shoulder bears the inscription, "ADAMS & JEFFERSON, JULY 4 A.D. 1776." American; 1826.*
COURTESY: The Corning Museum of Glass

Oddly enough, the word "booze" does not originate from
this Booz bottle, although the distiller could not have failed
to note and to capitalize on the happy coincidence. The
word "booze" actually comes from a French word.

Although an original Booz bottle is extremely difficult
to come by, there have been many reproductions of this
bottle, and it can be easily found in gift shops.

Thus, in a simple chronological perusal of liquor containers, there flows before us a panoramic view of a young
nation rising out of strife into a kind of superpatriotic phase
that lasted well into the nineteenth century.

18 One of the two remaining examples of the original Log Cabin bottles on record today. From the Wettlaufer Collection, Buffalo, New York, an olive-green glass with the inscription "TIPPECANOE" above the door on both sides of the bottle. Mount Vernon Glass Works, Mount Vernon, New York. 1840.

COURTESY: The Corning Museum of Glass

CHAPTER V

Medicinal Bottles

One of the biggest frauds ever perpetrated on the American public was the patent-remedy game.

Bitters and other patent-remedy bottles of this period are among the most avidly sought by modern collectors. In fact, much of the same fervor is found among collectors of bitters bottles that is evidenced among those who hunt down historical flasks.

The history of the bitters bottle goes back to the reign of George II when, in order to curb what had become excessive gin drinking on London streets, the king lowered a stiff tax on that popular commodity.

In order to stay in business—and satisfy the apparent needs of the public—gin sellers hit on the wonderful idea of seasoning their stock with a few herbal ingredients and labeling it "bitters," a tonic that was blatantly advertised to aid a variety of stomach upsets and disorders.

These herbs were oftentimes nothing more than a mild laxative, and the alcoholic content was practically the same as pure liquor.

Hard drinking had been on the increase in America, and by the mid-nineteenth century had begun to become a family problem. Workmen were pouring their money into the coffers of the distillers and bringing less and less of it home.

19 *A mold-blown aquamarine patent-medicine bottle with the original label intact. Note the applied lip.*
COURTESY: Old Sturbridge Village

When American women desperately embraced the concepts of the Women's Christian Temperance Union movement as an antidote to this problem, bitters again came to the rescue of the liquor dealers.

Taking their cue from their counterparts in England, distillers in America, masquerading as apothecaries, started seasoning their wares with herbal camouflage, and euphoria was again served in the name of science.

This led to a whole new line of home remedies, and each had its own unique place in everyday life in the United States.

This came at a time when people lived in constant fear of illness and were only too ready to believe that this or that bottled remedy would cure their ills, imagined and otherwise, and the fraud in some instances was a cruel one.

The public avidly soaked up the raucous advertising and eagerly attended medicine shows that pushed these specious products. It fell prey to its own fears of disease and depression and gullibly bought anything that was caramel-colored, strong-smelling, and packaged in a bottle. The sky-high alcoholic percentage of its contents only enhanced the so-called medicinal qualities of the bitter-tasting product.

Finally the Pure Food and Drug Law of 1906 brought an end to such shenanigans, and except for another brief try during Prohibition, the bitters binge died out.

In the meantime, bottle manufacturers came up with a whole new approach for the bitters, patent-remedy, and mineral-water bottle. Out went the sloping-shouldered flask shape and in came new forms and colors.

Their shapes were sometimes influenced by their contents. One of the most famous is a bottle in the shape of a bearded old man, made for Poland Springs Mineral Water. It is commonly known as "Moses at the Spring." Many fine copies have been made of this rather rare specimen.

"Brown's Celebrated Indian Herb Bitters" came in a bottle made in the form of an Indian princess. Other products were packaged in the form of everyday objects.

Characteristic colors for the bitters bottles were amber or brown in all shades from pale yellow through dark brown, and from olive to wine red. There were also aquamarine, green, blue, clear, and even puce.

Right alongside the bitters bottles were those that contained tonics, sarsaparillas, and cordials. Besides the usual liniments, cough remedies, painkillers, extracts, emulsions, elixirs, and syrups, appeared a never-ending variety of vermifuges, catarrh cures, scalp renovators, hair restorers, asthma remedies, and medicated gins.

Many collectors of these medicinal types are not content to collect single bottles of each type. Some go after examples of every brand and variety. Aside from the historical sidelights to be gleaned from this kind of series collecting, bottles in sets often command far better prices than the bottles would bring individually.

Although many of these medicinal types are not much to look at, they have generated a great deal of interest among collectors, new and old, and some of these bottles have even made it into museums.

20 *Medicinal-bitters bottle.*
COURTESY: Old Sturbridge Village

21 *Lemon-extract bottle dating around 1850, found with*
the label still intact.
COURTESY: Old Sturbridge Village

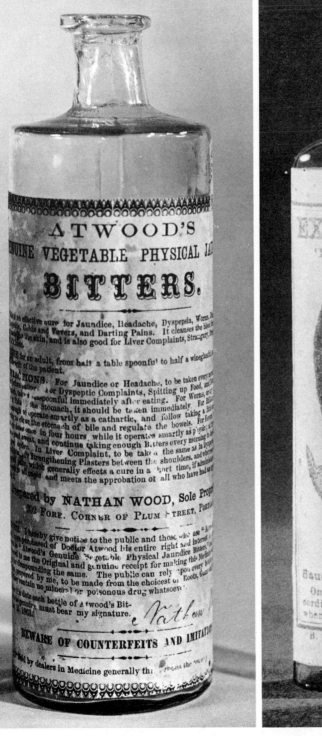

Of course medicine bottles go a long way back in the tale of civilization. Chinese opium bottles, no more than 1½ to 2 inches tall, filled a special need of the time. Although made of rather thick glass, they were easily shattered when dropped.

The Chinese came up with exquisite personal bottles that were indeed exotic and are among the most sought-after and expensive items for the collector. Snuff bottles of carved jade, in fantastically beautiful and intricate designs, are esthetically satisfying. But the price range of these bottles is out of the reach of the average collector.

Those interested in pharmaceutical bottles might well devote time to collecting the cobalt-blue poison bottles which first appeared in 1872, in a variety of sizes. These were manufactured by the Whitall-Tatum Company, which was succeeded by the H. B. Company.

Emptied of their grim contents, these bottles are exquisite in hue, if not distinguished by shapes. They were ordinary-looking round bottles, short-necked, and held from one half ounce to sixteen ounces.

There are other so-called poison bottles worthy of the collector's attention. Many of them are embossed with the standard warnings.

Poison bottles have not yet "caught on" with bottle collectors, but as the more familiar items are snapped up, many collectors will turn to this new field.

Perhaps some of the most exciting bottle hunting has taken place in some of the old western ghost towns in the United States. The gold miner of 1849 was a hardy sort of individual and often bereft of wife or family or other steadying influences. His daily consumption of alcoholic beverages is legend.

This, along with the fact that, for the most part, he lived out of a can and suffered poor indigestion because of diet deficiencies, accounts for the rich caches of liquor and patent-remedy bottles found in abandoned mines and towns.

Lemon extract was apparently high on the list of necessities, for it often filled both needs, being a strong but thoroughly drinkable alcoholic beverage. It also got around the laws of Prohibition, when needed, just as the bitters had.

A trip to one, or several, of these western ghost towns is a must for a serious collector. Take the family. It will be fun for everyone, for very seldom does one come back from these bottle hunts empty-handed, and the thrill of browsing through these dusty streets and crumbling shacks is reward in itself.

Miners usually buried their bottles in pits with their garbage and other trash. These dumping sites were often located in dense wooded areas, so as to get the stuff away from the living quarters, such as they were. Besides giving off unpleasant aromas in hot weather, refuse and garbage attracted insects and wild animals.

Old outhouses were also used for this purpose, and many a fine cache has been found in these crumbling lean-tos or in the immediate area.

Of course one must look for clues—pieces of broken glass or other signs of habitation, such as tin cans, pieces of dishes, etc.—and follow them to the dumping area. Creek beds are likely to yield many secrets, and fine bottle specimens. Creeks and streams were favorite dumping places.

So grubstake yourself to a trip out West. Make it a vacation. And while you're digging up bottles that will put some zing into your collection at home, try to soak up some of the history too.

Imagine yourself trudging wearily back to your solitary cabin after a hot, stifling, dusty day in the mine, a faithful dog your only company. Picture yourself rustling up a dreary supper of stew or beans, washed down with half a bottle of whiskey (or worse, lemon extract!). Then when you find that bottle, it will mean something to you.

CHAPTER VI

Household Bottles

In this category there is a veritable treasure trove of bottles serving hundreds of purposes.

It is also probably the richest category for the beginning collector to specialize in. Not only is this type of bottle a bit more accessible to the beginner and average collector, but household bottles encompass especially fascinating facets of life in the nineteenth and twentieth centuries in the United States.

Household bottles appeared in all kinds of shapes, sizes, and colors, and were dispensed by apothecaries and merchants in great quantities. They are also extremely difficult to identify sometimes, since one bottle was often used to hold several types of contents.

On the whole, the collector just beginning to become interested in acquiring bottles other than the back-yard variety will find this a relatively inexpensive field.

Sometimes the categories of medicinal and household bottles seem to overlap, as in mineral waters. The American people had great faith in the therapeutic qualities of mineral water, and they consumed immense quantities of the natural product.

These mineral-water bottles are distinctive and fun to collect. The early ones ranged from opaque to transparent and

22 "WASHINGTON SPRING, SARATOGA, N.Y.," emerald-green mineral-water bottle. Ht: 8".

23 A violet-blue pickle jar with vertical ribbing, produced by the Ravenna Glass Company, Ohio. Mold-blown. Early 1800s; Ht: 10½".
COURTESY: The Toledo Museum of Art

usually the name of the company and the contents were stamped in the bottle.

Among the first bottled spring waters was Saratoga Springs, followed by the popular Pluto mineral water. These certainly are the two names that rapidly come to mind when one thinks of mineral water and bottles.

Around 1845 came the soda-pop bottle. Effervescent drinks, on the order of Coca-Cola, Pepsi-Cola, and beer, were captured in opaque stone bottles with corks wired down to keep the contents from erupting forth. Later, thick glass bottles appeared.

The collector should give a great deal of thought to specializing in the various types found in the household field.

Aside from the mineral waters and soda-pop bottles there are the food containers. These include containers for sauces, jellies, pickles, honey, molasses, mustard, vinegar, catsup, oils, and other staples.

Some of these bottles inspired new designs, such as the beehive honey jars that appeared around 1900.

Food processors began to see a market in food packed in reusable containers. Catalogues of eighty years ago show many staple foods coming out in a variety of shapes, such as bottles that could be reused as vases and tableware. Several items appeared in these novelty bottles. It was a rich field for the food merchant then, and almost as rich a one for today's collector.

It seems strange to us now that only about sixty years ago milk was being carried about from house to house in a tin pail, and ladled out to consumers. This practice bothered Dr. Hervey D. Thatcher of Potsdam, New York, to the extent that he worked hard to alert the public to the need for milk bottles with sanitary caps. He patented such a cap in 1884.

It was not until pasteurization was called for on a large scale, however, that the returnable glass milk bottle came into its own. Bottlemakers began to mass-produce these bottles in the early 1900s. There were round and square milk bottles with a variety of sanitary seal caps.

For the collector looking for something a little different, there is the field of nursing bottles. There are about 180 years of glass infant feeders of constantly changing shapes and designs.

Other bottles in the household group are those that contained ammonia, hair dye, snuff, shoe blacking, and ink. The hair-dye bottles often carried the names of their makers and contents stamped in glass. Others carried this vital information on paper labels and were usually quite plain, although they came in several colors.

Snuff bottles were often quite fancy, sometimes cut from quartz or jade. In the earlier part of the nineteenth century, snuff was a commodity also used by ladies, and bottle manufacturers took this into account when they designed their glass containers.

24 *An olive-amber, blown, preserve jar possibly from the Pitkin Glassworks of East Hartford, Connecticut. 1783–1830; Ht: 8¼".*

COURTESY: The Toledo Museum of Art

25 *Another olive-amber, blown, preserve jar from the Frank-*
lin Glass Works of Warwick, Massachusetts. 1812–16; Ht:
11″.
COURTESY: The Toledo Museum of Art

26 A *pint-size, household bottle, mold-blown, with the in-*
scription, "J. B. WHEATLEY'S COMPOUND SYRUP,
DALLASBURGH, KY." 1850–70.

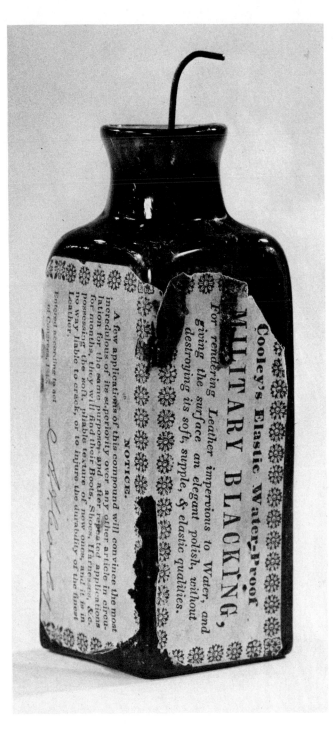

27　*Military blacking bottle claimed "INCREDULOUS . . .*
SUPERIORITY" for boots, shoes, harnesses.
COURTESY: Old Sturbridge Village

*28 Early household snuff bottle. Notice the blister imper-
fections in the glass.*
COURTESY: Old Sturbridge Village

Most of us remember the ink bottles that we used in school and which were filled from an even larger ink bottle. Usually, because of the literal indelibility of any negligence in this delicate task, only the most reliable pupils were given the coveted honor of filling inkwells. This, of course, was before the era of the ball-point pen.

We shouldn't leave this chapter without giving a nod to grenade and target bottles. They are unusual.

The grenade was actually a fire extinguisher. It was a ball-shaped glass bottle, usually five to eight inches high, and was filled with liquid. When the glass was hurled into the blaze, the bottle smashed and the liquid hopefully put out the fire.

The grenade fire extinguisher was patented in 1871 and was usually a richly designed bottle in diamond panels, sunbursts, monograms, or various kinds of ribbing. This quite rare bottle came in equally rich hues of amber, blue, green, olive green, and purple blue.

The target bottle—or shooting ball—was the forerunner of the clay pigeon and was patented in England in 1836. This was a glass ball 2½ or 3 inches wide, stuffed with feathers. It was tossed into the air and shot at with rifle or pistol. The first target bottles were smooth glass, but since bullets often ricocheted off of this surface, later balls were corrugated.

CHAPTER VII

Personal Bottles

At a time when daily bathing was a luxury, the importance of perfume and scent bottles could not be overestimated.

In journeys by stagecoach over hot, rugged terrain, and before deodorants came on the market, passengers often refreshed themselves with perfumes or colognes.

Ladies, making long trips by coach in close confinement with other passengers, often carried two flasks, one filled with cologne and the other with whiskey. In the course of such tedious journeys, it is conjectural as to which flask provided more comfort.

These flasks usually were the chestnut-type, holding about a half pint. Some of them may go as far back as Stiegel, but it is difficult to pinpoint them exactly.

During the nineteenth and twentieth centuries—during the era of close-fitting clothes and stays—women relied very much on smelling salts and ammonia snifters. Some of these were packaged in most appealing scent bottles, some cut glass.

Double-scent bottles of the late nineteenth century, combined two bottles in one. One side of the double bottle offered the resuscitating scent of ammonia, while the other contained an essence of some sweet-smelling flower.

Many of these double-scent bottles were very ornate and

some were small works of art, containing jewels embedded in silver or gold.

The double-scent came in several shapes. Sometimes the two bottles looked like one oblong one with a cap at each end; sometimes the two bottles were hinged; sometimes they shared a common side.

Whatever the shapes of these intriguing bottles, it is always worth a few hurrahs when one of them is found.

CHAPTER VIII

Decanters and Figurals

Decanters have a long history, used in almost every civilization from the first made in Egypt in 1500 B.C. to the present time.

Before liquors came in "packaged" form, decanters were needed to transfer whiskey and wine from tavern to home. The decanter was a necessary accouterment to gracious living and entertaining.

The first decanters were simple containers with a purely functional purpose. Early "seal" bottles were personalized and prized by prestige-conscious men of means.

Although it is not certain when decanters were first made in America, handsome carafes are known to have been made by Stiegel in the 1770s. He produced them in many colors—including his famous blues and purples—and in sizes ranging from gills to quarts. One clear-glass decanter, attributed to Stiegel, is on display at the Metropolitan Museum of Art in New York.

Many of the decanters being made at several glasshouses in the mid-eighteenth and mid-nineteenth centuries imitated the beautiful Irish cut-glass products that had met with such favor in the New World. In fact, even experts have difficulty in identifying some decanters made overseas and those made by American artisans. "American Waterford" became a household name in glass.

29, 30, 31, 32, 33, 34, 35 *Decorative decanters produced by the James B. Beam Distilling Company of Kentucky.*
COURTESY: James B. Beam Distilling Company

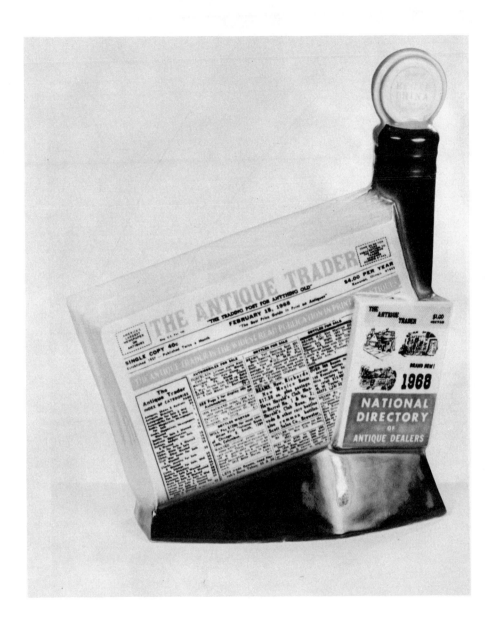

Thus decanters have been part of the American way of life for some time.

Among the most collectible of modern-day holiday gift decanters are those produced, since 1953, by the James B. Beam Distilling Company. The prices commanded by Beam bottles are considerable, as indicated in the chapter on bottle pricing. There is no doubt that they represent a solid investment for the collector, besides providing many a conversation piece.

In fact, the prices on these bottles vary so from state to state, and from locality to locality, that it is common practice for cross-country truck drivers to stock up on Beam bottles obtainable in one city and take them for resale to another where prices are higher.

These ceramic bottles in vibrant colors, depict everything from cherubs to Cleopatra. Some of the subjects include the Alaska Centennial, cats, cable cars, hippies, California redwoods, flowers, Mark Antony, the Pony Express, Spanish matadors, the Seattle World's Fair, Harolds Club in Reno, and Yosemite National Park, to name only a few.

They are made to hold Kentucky Straight Bourbon, and sometimes the prices are the same whether they are filled with liquor or not, especially when one finds an antique shop next to a package store. So, for contents' sake, try the liquor store first.

Another group of bottles that were often reused for decanters because of their novel effect or propaganda value, are the figurals.

A figural is a bottle wholly made in the form of a human figure, animal, or some common object. This differentiates it from the decorated bottle on which faces or figures were molded in relief.

One of the most difficult of these figurals to find is the so-called "pig" bottle. This bottle, made in the shape of a

36 *Bitters bottles are found in all shapes and sizes, even to*
this porker. Philbrook & Tucker of Boston was the distribu-
tor of this "SUFFOLK BITTERS."
COURTESY: Old Sturbridge Village

pig, with the contents poured forth from the pig's bottom, commands large prices today.

Other figurals were made in the shape of people, animals, and objects which included fish, bullfighters, bears, revolvers, sea shells, violins, whales, parrots, the Bunker Hill Monument, and George Washington and Zachary Taylor.

Some of these were used for perfumes, some for candy, soft drinks, household ammonia, or syrups. Many were used to accommodate several types of contents.

The invention of the bottlemaking machine made all of this possible, and bottlemakers competed with each other in producing the most intricate molds possible.

CHAPTER IX

Collaterals

Collectors often find interesting sidelights to their hobby.

One of these is the collecting of collateral material that helps to bring alive the era in which certain bottles were made and used.

The most vivid material can be found in the colorful forms of advertising that expounded and accompanied the marvelous curative powers of the various patent remedies.

These included slogans and testimonies that appeared in the magazines of the day. There were blatant signs showing healthy pretty girls, songs, poems, and several kinds of gimmicks.

They had the traditional twofold purpose of the advertising game: to attract attention and to urge purchase. They did both very well, apparently, with everything from hair restorers to vermifuges.

These gaudy works of art appeared everywhere, unashamedly hawking their suspicious wares to a gaping public that found them irresistible.

Many of the multicolored cards can still be found in cellars or attics, lying undisturbed in the dust among other forgotten relics.

If you don't happen to know anyone with a real dusty attic, try the antique shops. This kind of memorabilia can still be found in abundance in shops and in old general country stores.

Along with the handbills, wrappers, signs, and cards that advertised these patent-remedy products, there is other good material to add to your collection. Old political buttons or editorial cartoons, newspaper clips, almanacs, paperweights; anything that sniffs of a particular era is acceptable.

The main thing is that it enhance—and does not detract from—your bottles. When you find just the right thing, display it, right alongside your collection.

Collaterals—and this does not mean "clutterals"—of the right kind can greatly enhance any bottle collection, and it will help make your bottles more meaningful to collectors and non-collectors alike.

CHAPTER X

The Mason Jar

―――――

Until the nineteenth century there were few attempts to preserve food. Louis Pasteur, whose discoveries led to milk preservation by the process that was later to use his name, also made possible the preservation of food by heating and sterilization.

It is easy for us to take for granted the familiar screw-on-top Mason jar, but the first bottles used for this purpose were rather pathetic, for no proper seal against air had yet been devised. Early cork seals were scarcely any seal at all.

However, with the invention of the Mason jar in 1858, home preserving became a practical reality. Right from the start, it was a booming success. Indeed, it revolutionized the care and feeding of the world.

Given an airtight seal and a workable method of home canning, housewives were able to vary their families' winter fare of squash, potatoes, and turnips with succulent delights from the summer's garden. The Mason jar—and its successor, the Ball jar with the locked hinge—made possible a groaning board laden with juicy tomatoes, peaches and pears, string beans, chili sauce, and pickles.

Home canning became common practice, and a skill most housewives were expected to cultivate for the betterment of their husbands and families. Neighbors were quick to sympathize with a man whose wife did not "can."

37 *A handmade, aqua-colored jar manufactured by Ball Brothers Company Incorporated sometime during the 1890– 1905 period.*
COURTESY: Ball Corporation

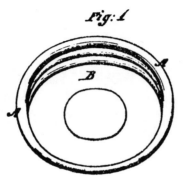

38 Lewis R. Boyd's patent in 1896, shown in these two figures, provided a glass liner for the zinc cap and in this manner prevented corrosion.

THE SMALLEY FRUIT JAR.

BEAUTY. CHEAPNESS.

SIMPLICITY. RELIABILITY.

MASON'S PATENT NOV. 30TH 1858

THE SMALLEY FRUIT-JAR PAT. SEP. 23. 84

MASON'S IMPROVED.

Every Jar Made Extra Heavy
and Warranted to Seal.

38A Early trade mark that distinguished Mason jars of 1800s.

38B The glass jar-making machine patented in 1898 by F. C. Ball. This was one of the first semiautomatic machines to go into operation in this country and it gradually replaced the glass blower who worked with individual hand-held molds. The first fully automatic glass machines came into use in the early 1900s.

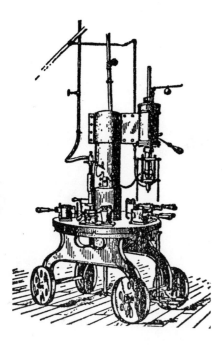

John Mason's basic idea of a molded-glass jar with a threaded top has undergone several modifications over the years, but the so-called Mason jar of today is essentially the same one for which the inventor applied for patent in 1858.

Ironically, Mason was not to benefit from his remarkable invention. In 1873 he assigned his patent rights to a fruit-jar company with which he had become associated. When the patent rights expired, other glass factories began to manufacture the Mason jar.

By 1887 the Ball Bros. Glass Mfg. Co. at Muncie, Indiana, was putting out 600,000 jars daily. These were known as "Ball-Mason" jars, and the Ball company continued to develop the product. These developments related to designs for the jar itself and the machinery with which to manufacture it, and the Ball company secured numerous patents.

Although his invention of the preserve jar left an indelible imprint on American daily life, and although he invented and patented several other items unrelated to bottles or jars, Mason gained little in the way of monetary value, and died a poor man. As with many ingenious men, he didn't seem to achieve the necessary "carry through" so important in business ventures.

However, the glass jar that holds so securely the goodies of the summer's harvest and is still placed so proudly and lovingly on countless tables across the nation, and continents as well, will probably always be known simply as the "Mason" jar.

CHAPTER XI

Closures

_____

As early as 600 B.C., man looked about for some means to stop or plug his bottles. Without a satisfactory seal of some sort, the contents leaked and were contaminated by the elements and outside agents.

The bottle collector should give at least a cursory glance at this facet of his hobby, for it adds still another dimension to it.

In early times a variety of materials was used to seal bottles: straw dipped in wax, gobs of clay, leather, anything, in fact, that would even halfway do the job. Unfortunately, that's just about all the job any of these so-called closures succeeded in doing. It was all rather makeshift, and certainly far from satisfactory, and the stuff had a habit of falling into the contents of the bottle when being removed or replaced.

Probably the earliest closure that worked at all was cork. It dates back centuries before existing corks we know to have been used in the late eighteenth century. In fact, cork was such a good stopper that it is still in widespread use today.

There were two things against the use of cork as a closure. First, it took some trouble to remove it; usually a corkscrew or some similar tool was needed at hand. Second, it had to be kept wet or it would dry out, and no amount of skill or mechanical aid would remove it then, except in fragments which left unappetizing bits floating about in the contents of the bottle, if, indeed, it could be removed at all.

In 1860 Hiram Codd, an Englishman, came up with one of the first steps in developing a satisfactory seal for soda-water or "pop" bottles. His invention consisted of a rubber ring which was supported by a special groove within the bottle itself. Before the rubber ring was fitted to this groove in the neck of the bottle, a marble was dropped into the opening. A seal was achieved when pressure, created by the contents, pressed the marble against the rubber ring.

There were a couple of serious drawbacks to this device. It was necessary to fill the bottle upside down, and every time the bottle was raised or lowered, as it would be in drinking or pouring, the marble had a tendency to rush in and plug the hole.

The latter difficulty was circumvented by placing a second rubber ring in the neck of the bottle. Although the device was condemned by health authorities as unsafe, this did not prevent its widespread use for a time.

Twelve years later, William Hutchinson invented an internal stopper that had a wire loop on one end and a rubber disc on the other. The rubber disc served as a seal within the neck of the bottle, but careless handling of the wire loop could easily break the seal. It was likewise condemned by the health authorities.

A few years later the gravitating stopper made an appearance. It, too, was an internal stopper, employing a rubber disc or washer which was forced against the neck by the pressure, created by the contents of the bottle. Again, health authorities failed to give approval. The bottles were hard to clean, and the closures often picked up dirt.

All of these early stoppers—in spite of their ingenious invention—were considered unsanitary, as well as impractical for mass production.

However, an important milestone in finding a practical and foolproof seal was the so-called lightning stopper designed by Charles de Quillefeldt in 1875. The stopper itself was usually porcelain which was anchored to a rubber ring by wire. The idea was patented in 1878 and is actually still being used today.

In the last half of the nineteenth century, thousands of bottle stoppers were designed and many of them patented, and that's about the last that was heard of them.

In 1892 William Painter came up with his startling metal crown seal. It fulfilled all the needs of the commercial bottling industry, and it is practically the same metal seal we see today on soda-pop and beer bottles. It took Painter ten years to develop it, but when it came along, the metal seal was an instant success.

A collector of bottles could well turn his attention to this fascinating field. A more detailed study on this subject would yield many additional items of interest to the bottle lore of the serious collector. It would also be a service to fellow bottle collectors.

CHAPTER XII

Insulators

One sideline to bottle collecting, which started as a kind of fad a few years ago and now has begun to reach mania proportions, involves glass insulators.

What insulators have to do with bottle collecting isn't quite clear, but it seems that by virtue of a basic interest in all things glass, plus a certain temperament geared to hunting and digging, the bottle enthusiast finds a fascination in these heavy glass "cups" that is difficult to define.

I can only say that the first time I went to an antique shop in search of old bottles, I came out carrying two insulators—one Brookfield and one Hemingray—which I had bought for seventy-five cents apiece, and I could hardly wait to get them home. They are standing on the window sill in the study. They are useful as paperweights, and they are grand conversation pieces. I'm still trying very hard not to get interested in them because I said in the very beginning that I would never collect insulators, and here are these two constantly picking at me to go out and get some more.

Insulators, as most of us probably know, were used to insulate telephone wires before the days of sheathed cables. I am told by a representative of the local telephone company that some of these old glass relics are still in use in some country areas.

39 Glass insulators, although native to all parts of the country, are increasingly difficult to find. Their value may range up to $100.

left to right.

The Corning Pyrex-style insulator of carnival glass; notice the saddle groove cut across the dome.

Cable-style "Roman Helmet," aqua.

Knowles Cable with saddle top, aqua.

Transposition style, a two-piece insulator, the top of which lifts off.

Chicago Insulator Company, blue, valued at $50 to $100, unusual for its six irregular depressions, two of which can be seen on either side.

CR: J. F. Hartwell Collection

When I was in grade school I remember boys pitching rocks at the blue-green glass blobs on the telephone wires, or shooting them with BB guns.

Telephone companies are amused and delighted by "guilt" letters containing small sums of money that come in occasionally from some of those boys, now grown men, who for some reason feel compelled to pay for this small crime of childhood.

Most glass insulators are of a cylindrical or "petticoat" shape. These basic shapes, however, have an astonishing number of variations which make them easily identifiable. These distinguishing characteristics are included in the types and numbers of "threads," "skirts," and "drip points." The latter refers to the beads or "points" around the bottom of the insulator, the purpose of which was to shed moisture from the insulator before it could get inside and cause trouble.

Insulators differ also in color (green, aqua, clear, amethyst), and many are embossed with company names and dates. Types of tapers, ridges, grooves, domes, etc., also help with identification.

Telephone insulators go back to 1876, and they were used on telegraph wires as early as 1844.

Part of the lure of insulator collecting is an interest in the past, a past at least part of which many of us can still remember.

Because of the demand, insulators are becoming standard items in many antique shops and so-called "junk" shops. Sometimes back-yard or garage sales are sources of supply.

For those who like to hunt out their own, the best place to look is where they are most apt to be, along overhead telephone lines and also where these lines used to be. When insulators were replaced, the telephone company often left them around the bases of poles or on crossarms.

Pound for pound, insulators aren't worth a great deal in-

40   *Hemingray glass insulators are a more contemporary collectible than the Brookfield; they generally have a lower value when buying or selling. This display clearly shows the drip points, a Hemingray innovation aimed at diverting water from the wire lines and thus eliminating short circuits. Glass drip points are to be found on older models. Glass is either clear or aqua.*

CR: Constance Casella Collection

trinsically. Prices run generally from $.50 to $3.00, depending on rarity, condition, and age. Some in the rare category may climb to $10, $20, even $30. But there were millions of these glass cups made and used, and at the present time, at least, the main interest in them among collectors is esthetic rather than financial. As public interest grows and is nurtured (as, indeed, it will be), prices can be expected to go up for more desired specimens.

Some insulators are rather handsome, and since they are such wonderful conversation pieces, the collector will want to display at least a few of his best ones for the edification and enjoyment of his friends, many of whom probably don't know an insulator when they see one.

As in bottle display, this calls for a bit of imagination.

Light, of course, is very important. Thick glass insulators look their best with light streaming right through them.

Simple groupings are always effective. However, if the collector is able to relate his specimens to the present, it will be even more satisfying. He might trace back some of his insulators to a certain area of the country in which they were used, and the dates of their use. Old photographs of the period can usually be obtained. Or perhaps an artist friend can work up a couple of sketches for a background.

For the more ambitious, a small diorama, with small poles and telephone lines and model houses or a horse-and-buggy, will help re-create the scene in which a particular insulator was used. This could be a challenging project for the clever teen-ager in the family.

If one likes to look at these odd shapes of glass and wonder about the days when they helped carry messages across a still-young nation, all kinds of display ideas should start springing forth. The main thing is for the collector to try to communicate his own enthusiasm to the observer.

So grab yourself a little chunk of another era.

CHAPTER XIII

What Are Your Bottles Worth?

Pricing bottles is a ticklish business. To find out what any particular bottle is worth on the market, the best way is to go to a reputable antique-bottle dealer and ask him.

Bottle prices go up and down like the proverbial seesaw, and it is folly to try to come up with any kind of definitive work on the subject.

The best we can do is to give a broad idea of how prices run generally for certain types and categories of bottles. For specific, up-to-date information, one's best bet is to pick up the latest antiques price list. At least one of these is available at most public libraries.

Of course, as one reads bottle books and becomes more aware of the complete world of bottles, and as one browses through antique shops, it will soon become apparent that certain kinds of bottles and certain periods in bottle history command better prices than others.

Although there is no crime in buying reproductions of famous bottles (historical flasks, for example), the collector who knows better will pass up a gleaming, polished copy in the gift shop when he can buy an original bottle for maybe a dollar and a half more in an antique shop next door.

Reproductions of bottles have their place in a collection, just as fine reproductions of antique furniture have their place in the home. The collector owes it to himself to acquaint himself with bottle lore so that he knows when he is buying a reproduction, at reproduction prices.

The collector who has just begun to want to learn more about his hobby, and who is getting ready to invest money as well as time and labor in his collection, would do well to see all the fine old bottles that he can. No better place to start is the Corning Glass Museum in Corning, New York. It is necessary to see some of these old bottles before we can with any degree of consistency recognize reproductions.

Desirable as some reproductions are, there's nothing quite like the feel in the hand of an old flask that has survived the roughest kind of treatment over the years.

It's a pity old bottles can't speak. Take that old Eagle flask. Did it ride the hip of some rugged frontiersman as his horse's hoofs thundered across the plains? Was it used to wash down a supper of biscuits and beans and bitter coffee, and was it passed round the fire from hand to hand to help ward off the chill of night?

Or perhaps it accompanied its owner to heated political meetings, or family picnics, or perhaps it simply just spelled plain old hospitality when gentlemen gathered for a game of cards.

Yes, it is very difficult to put a price tag on a bottle that twits the imagination. But it is only natural to want to know what our bottles are worth on the market, and so here we will try to come up with a few guidelines.

First of all, it is not likely that the bottles we have been digging up in our back yard are going to be either old enough or rare enough to be worth much.

Even some fairly old bottles, including those with embossing (contents or manufacturer's name stamped in glass), won't be worth much more than a few dollars.

41 *Golden-amber pint flask inscribed, "BALTIMORE, GLASS WORKS," 1850s.*
COURTESY: The Corning Museum of Glass

42 *Yellow-green pint flask, probably from the Pittsburgh area. Obverse shows the portrait of Andrew Jackson; reverse has flowers. 1824–40.*
COURTESY: The Corning Museum of Glass

43 A quart-size, pale blue-green, circular flask with concentric rings and a small eagle on one side and concentric rings with the inscription "NGCo" on the other side. Probably New England Glass Company, Cambridge, Massachusetts. 1818–25.

COURTESY: The Corning Museum of Glass

44   *Deep amethyst chestnut-type pocket flask probably made by the Manheim Glassworks of Henry William Stiegel. It was blown in a diamond-daisy-pattern mold. 1765–74; Ht: 13 cm.*
COURTESY: The Corning Museum of Glass

One must also remember that the market price quoted would be that paid by another collector. A dealer will probably pay half or even less than half the amount, since he buys with the intention of resale.

If in your digging, you find embossed bottles or free-blown bottles (the latter will have irregular features and no seam), you will be getting into the range of bottles worth between $2.00 to $5.00. Some will be worth much more.

The rule of thumb is this: before selling or giving away any old free-blowns or embossed bottles, check antique-bottle price lists or get a price from a knowledgeable antique dealer or fellow collector. This rule cannot be emphasized too much.

Suppose we list some in this better-price category of the uncommon but common sort of bottle you are likely to hit upon in digging or trading.

In the free-blown whiskey and wine types, look for sheared tops and rough pontil marks (*see* Glossary of Terms). Some of these bottles will be in the $20 to $30 class.

Some of the oval, tapered-at-the-bottom flasks command prices from $3.00 to $10.

Bitters bottles, especially those stamped in glass, can be found in the $5.00 to $8.00 range. But they can also be worth much more.

Now we begin to see the intricacies involved in pricing. For example, one expert source lists Dr. J. Hostetter's Stomach Bitters in *amber* at $6.00 to $8.00. But last year a Hostetter's Bitters in *green* was sold for $40!

As with everything else, antique-bottle pricing is contingent on the simple law of supply and demand.

Let's take another example: DeWitt's Stomach Bitters in *brown* is listed at $5.00 to $7.00. In *amber* it recently sold for $55!

We can readily see that prices vary for brand, variety, color of glass, and the condition of the bottle itself. Effective pricing needs to be done on an individual bottle basis. However, we can still arrive at average figures for certain groups.

Most of the really old and rare bottles, such as the seal bottles, and those wares produced in the American colonies and just after the Revolutionary War, are already in museums or private collections.

However, it is possible, in some antique shops or through some bottle dealers, to pick up a really old bottle of late seventeenth- or eighteenth-century vintage for about $100. If you find one, it is money well spent.

Historical flasks command good prices generally, but the chasm between one variety and another is awesome. Ordinarily these flasks run from $20 to $60.

Some of the early sunbursts run to $75, and some of the Masonics to $135.

The gap in pricing is even more severe in the figurals. Here is covered a range from $3.00 to $35, with many listed at much more, including the famous fish bottle in amber for Dr. Fish's Bitters. This recently sold for $130.

A couple of the most sought-after bottles are the so-called "Travelers Companion" (which recently sold for $350) and some of the Pike's Peak bottles. One of the latter with an eagle, stars, and "My Country" on the reverse just sold for $310.

But these prices are rare—as are the bottles which bring them—and the average bottle collector can best prepare himself for buying, selling, and trading items in his collection by carefully studying the annual antiques price lists, by talking with dealers and other collectors, and by studying bottles and bottle history. If we repeat ourselves on this score, it is only because it is so very important.

The Beam bottles mentioned in an earlier chapter represent a hard-core investment. These bottles seem to rocket year after year.

For the most part, Beam bottles fall into the $10 to $60 range with a liberal sprinkling of prices in between that rather wide gap. Some of them are worth a lot more.

Because of the popularity of these unusual ceramic bottles, let us look at several of the more valuable items and what they were recently bought and sold for:

Sante Fe, 1960	$200.
West Virginia, 1963	150.
Man in Barrel, 1958	275.
Ram, 1958	95.
Cat, 1967	250.
Harolds Club, Nevada, gray	225.
Harrahs, Nevada, gray	525.

In the space of only a few years the Beam bottle has established a tradition, and it attracts the attention of collectors and speculators alike.

Mason preserve jars are also collectible items. The aqua jars embossed "Mason's Patent Nov. 30th 1858" are worth about $5.00 to $7.00. On the base of some of these jars appears "Pat. Nov. 26, 67."

In this same price range are jars embossed "Mason's Improved," with the same base stamping as the jars mentioned above. Other Mason jars bring similar prices.

Ink bottles are another category where prices fluctuate wildly. The common types of twenty or thirty years ago are worth anywhere from $2.00 to $8.00 ordinarily. A three-piece molded olive-green bottle embossed with "Ward's Ink" recently sold for about $13.50.

Another ink bottle, "Mr. and Mrs. Carter," was recently listed at $35; and still another, "Whitefriars," with pink,

45 Inkwells

top row, left to right.

Dark olive-green, Stoddard, New Hampshire, about 1830.

Clear, mold-blown, attributed to Whitney Glass Works, Glassboro, New Jersey, about 1840.

Large, olive-green, Stoddard, New Hampshire, about 1830.

bottom row, left to right.

Light green, Coventry, Connecticut, about 1830.

Dark olive, quilted-diamond pattern, Stoddard, New Hampshire, about 1830.

Low profile, dark olive, Stoddard, New Hampshire, about 1830.

COURTESY: The Toledo Museum of Art

blue, and white canes and a beehive stopper is listed at $250!

Household bottles were produced in great quantities. Most of these, which held an endless variety of contents, are found in the $.75 to $3.00 range.

One reason for price fluctuations is the fact that antiques, and this includes old bottles, sell at different prices in various parts of the United States, or, for that matter, the world.

So again we are back to the question: What is a bottle worth?

The only sure way we can tell the real worth of any bottle is to find out what someone else is willing to pay for it. Obviously a collector who is trying to fill a gap in a series of bottles will pay a few dollars more for a bottle than its so-called "worth." But this is the moment of truth—when we try to sell.

One category of bottles we haven't discussed much are snuff bottles. Many of these were of quite intricate design and richly ornamented. They came in crystal, ivory, jade, lapis lazuli, porcelain, mother-of-pearl, and milk glass.

Today they bring very high prices. Recently a jade snuff bottle, decorated with bird and plum blossoms, on a teak stand, was sold for $495. Several others have been bought and sold in recent months for over $200.

In determining the age of bottles, one should observe the lips, collars, and pontil marks. Another method is easy to remember and quite useful.

Before 1860 the mold seam ran up the side of the bottle, extending just over the shoulder. On bottles made between 1860 and 1880 the mold seam runs a good way up the neck. Between 1880 and 1890 the seam extends the length of the bottle, but not through the lip. On any bottle made after 1900 the mold seam extends the full length of the bottle and up and over the lip as well.

Although relatively few bottles are worth a great deal of money, the important thing is to remember that a bottle collection is unique in itself. Each bottle represents a chunk of frozen time. How does one price that?

Besides, there is always the chance that one of these days your shovel will clink against a real discovery—maybe one that could end up in a museum.

Now wouldn't that be something!

CHAPTER XIV

Where to Start Hunting

Now that we have a better idea of the world of bottles, of their relation to the everyday and historical events of this and other eras, and now that we have an inkling of what some of these bottles are worth, we are ready to get down to the delightful business of searching them out.

Most of us bottle hunters won't run into old and rare bottles right off. For a while we may have to be contented with the back-yard types, and most of the ones we find in the immediate neighborhood will be most of the simple trash variety: non-returnable soft-drink and beer bottles, whiskey and wine bottles, and innumerable household containers.

However, one must start somewhere, and the non-returnables and household bottles of today, which are being tossed away and generally ignored, will be the collectibles of tomorrow.

First we want to get together samples of the common bottles of today; then we can pursue the older and rarer types. This will be a good training period for us, and an exciting one.

So before we throw *any* bottle away, let's take a good second look at it. Will its image in an antiques catalogue twenty years from now haunt you because you tossed it aside?

Clear out a place in the basement or prepare a special section in the attic or other room of your house to accommodate your collection. Then start your hunt.

Start with the bottles in your grocery bag or the family refrigerator. When you have these cleaned, polished, classified, and put on the shelf, it will spur you on to do more.

Don't pass up anything: pickle and olive bottles, catsup bottles, vinegar bottles, pepper-sauce and Worcestershire-sauce bottles, molasses and syrup bottles, mustard bottles, steak-sauce bottles, ammonia bottles, onion-juice bottles, you-name-it bottles.

This is the way we began, and we didn't find it such a humble beginning. We found a real glass milk bottle in our refrigerator to start with. How many of us can say that today? With plastics making inroads everywhere in the packaging industry, and with so many bottles being destroyed by wholesale means daily, there is no such thing as a too-common glass household bottle.

One thing is very important. Try to develop the habit of labeling everything, before you have a chance to forget it. Label every bottle according to date, where found or obtained, and original contents. You will soon find that there are some bottles that have served several purposes. When this comes to light, be sure to make a note of it. Among other things, it will save you from making duplication.

When we first moved into our house in Weymouth, Massachusetts, we soon found a large patch of ground in the back area that was full of rather mean briars, you know, the kind that reach out to you when you try to step by, and poke holes in slacks and stockings. So for several days we spent long hours digging them up by the roots, hitting rocks and bits of flying glass as we went along.

Soon it became apparent that this had been used for a dumping area at one time. Under beds of rotting leaves and root-entangled rocks, we came up with several old bottles that were still intact.

They were crusty with dirt and clay and all kinds of mineral deposits, but we spent many days soaking, cleaning, and polishing them. It was a happy time.

The collector—especially the beginner—will find that the intrinsic worth of bottles is not always of primary concern. But when one finds an interesting-looking specimen in the earth, it's like finding a penny in a box of nails. It is a pleasant surprise, and one instinctively looks for more.

Once we have graduated from the back yard, our neighbors' yards, and the town dump, we are ready to tackle the outside world.

It is important to ask permission first before digging on private property. It not only keeps us out of trouble, it can, at times, lead to new discoveries. Public dumping grounds are good sources, but browsers are not always encouraged because of the obvious dangers present. You'll enjoy your digging more if you know you aren't trespassing.

As we go along, we soon see that as soon as our eyes are alert to them, bottles pop up everywhere: along the highway, in empty fields, along riverbanks, at the seashore, in abandoned places of all kinds. Back alleys in the city sometimes yield interesting specimens.

Woods near living areas are good places to look, for people often used to dump trash away from their living quarters, and the woods provided a discreet hiding place for such eyesores.

Generally these trash heaps were buried, and we need to keep out a sharp eye for the clues that lead us to these areas. Well-traveled paths with tiny offshoot trails sometimes lead to rich finds.

Cans and broken glass are always signs of more, either near or underground. When we come to a likely area, we

46   The result of a morning's picnic in the woods. It's a matter of luck to come up with such a variety in one place.
CR: Photograph by Christa König

must remember to dig carefully, layer by layer, so as not to damage any specimens that might still be in one piece.

One way of recognizing these dumping places is by the somewhat noticeable depressions left in the ground as the dirt and rubbish settled.

Sometimes these pits go down as far as eight feet, and some beautiful old bottles have been taken from them. There will often be several of these dumping stations in the same wooded area, for they were usually used over a fairly long stretch of time.

Caches of old bottles are often "psyched out" simply by remembering that one problem that has followed people in any civilization, wherever they moved or lived, was the ever-present one of trash disposal.

It was only a few years ago that people put their rubbish out on the street and the county hauled it away. Until then it was every man for himself, and the householder developed some ingenious methods for getting rid of his refuse and keeping it out of sight.

By pretending we are a householder of the same era, we can imagine where some of these out-of-sight, out-of-mind hiding places might be.

It was usual to dump refuse into creeks, ditches, and crevices or ravines of any kind. Sometimes a certain patch near the outside corner of the property was designated for that purpose.

47   *This could happen when one's enthusiasm gets out of control. Dig carefully not to break any of the hidden treasures.*
CR: Photograph by Christa König

48   Among the finds of this particular afternoon are a Brook-field insulator and an amethyst bottle.
CR: Photograph by Christa König

Stone walls and fences were often good camouflages. Walking alongside both sides of these fences and keeping an eye out for pieces of metal and porcelain and glass will sometimes bring something to light.

Old cellar holes and septic tanks are other likely areas in which bottles of some vintage can be found.

So get on the hiking boots, provision the crew with some good-size sandwiches and plenty of cold drinks, and don't do what we did on our first bottle-hunting expedition—forget to bring a sack in which to carry back the treasure!

CHAPTER XV

Some Tips on Cleaning Bottles

The thrill of finding a good vintage bottle that has been buried in the earth for perhaps decades can only be matched by seeing the crusty debris fall away, revealing the hidden beauty beneath.

There are several methods for cleaning bottles. Each collector will eventually find his own favorite short cuts.

First of all, most bottles will need a good soaking, sometimes for several days, before clay and mineral deposits come loose. Some people use lye—a caustic and somewhat dangerous solution to have lying around—and some are partial to a solution of sudsy ammonia and water. There are other soaks, but these are probably the most common.

Whatever solution you decide to use, *never* use a combination of bleach and any acid (such as vinegar or toilet-bowl cleaner). This combination releases a highly poisonous chlorine gas. It is better to stay away from household bleaches altogether, for many of us are not always aware of what solutions are acid.

You will need a very large metal tub or other container in which to soak a number of bottles at one time.

Get as much of the crust off the bottles before putting

49 Bottles should be soaked in a solution of ammonia and
water, or simply a strong detergent solution to loosen encrusted dirt. Strong solutions of lye or bleach are not recom-
mended. Beware of mixing acids and bleach.
CR: Photograph by Christa König

them in to soak. And remember, during this sometimes
touchy operation of cleaning, patience will be important.
Mother Nature takes her time. It took years for the dirt to
get on those bottles; it isn't all going to come off in five
minutes.

After a few days the encrustations should yield to a good
scrubbing with steel wool and plenty of soap or detergent.
A stiff bottle brush comes in handy too.

50   *Use a stiff bottle brush to get at the sediment inside the bottle.*
CR: Photograph by Christa König

If the brush isn't able to thoroughly clean the inside of the bottle, partly fill the bottle with water and add a handful of coarse sand and a few pebbles. Then shake—but not too vigorously, or you may break the bottle! This gentle abrasive action should grind away what's left.

A good rinse in warm water and a loving polish with a soft cloth should result in a gleaming and proud addition to your collection.

CHAPTER XVI

Displaying Your Bottles

———

A bottle collection can be a thing of beauty, or it can become just another dust-catching junk heap.

Bottles should be displayed with the same loving care and enthusiasm with which they were hunted, dug up, cleaned, and polished.

Some of them, indeed, are works of art and superb craftsmanship, and now their second lives, in a sense, are about to begin. Here they are, to beautify the present with the glories of a rich past.

Bottles catch dust; there's no denying it. To combat this natural state of affairs, some collectors store their bottles in cabinets. For a very large collection, specially constructed shelves and cabinets will be needed.

If bottles must be put in a wooden cabinet, do use one of light-colored wood. Otherwise the bottles will blend into the woodwork. Glass doors, of course, are essential.

How to display a collection of bottles depends pretty much on what the collector hopes to achieve as a final result.

Is the collection valuable? Do you want people handling your bottles? What kind of display do the bottles themselves seem to suggest? Is your main interest accessibility, or do you want your bottles to add a spot of beauty to your home?

Perhaps you may be satisfied merely to place a few glass-encased shelves in front of a window. This simple display in the right kind of room can be quite effective, and the bottles are always easily accessible for cataloguing and for showing to collector friends.

On the other hand, if you want to really show off the beauty of your bottles (and we hope you do!), then get with it, and don't spare the imagination! Let it really soar!

First you must decide whether you want your bottles enclosed or out in the open where they can be readily examined. There are two things against the latter. One, they will have to be cleaned often, and two, they are easily knocked over or dropped.

A cabinet, on the other hand—even a glass cabinet—hides them from view to some extent.

Either way, though, your bottles can be displayed in such a way as to enhance their individual characteristics.

If you feel better about keeping your treasures in a glass cabinet—and you will certainly want to do this with the more valuable items—be sure that they are backlighted or sidelighted by an adjacent window.

Glass, being a translucent or transparent and highly reflective material, needs plenty of light to show it off.

In massing several bottles together on one shelf, strive for order and harmony between the basic shapes. A tall bottle followed by a short one and then a tall one, and so on, stringing along a shelf, keeps the eye jumping all over the place and is a far from pleasing arrangement.

Just as in arranging any "still life," tall, thin objects should be put toward the back and be flanked or partially surrounded by shorter, squatter objects. The tall one then becomes a focal point on which to rest the eye while observing all the bottles. "A hen and her chickens" is always a safe pleasing arrangement.

Do experiment with various arrangements until you find

the ones you like. Bottles shouldn't be strung along a shelf like clay pigeons. They should be arrayed in groupings, each one its own little tableau, so to speak.

Another way of effectively displaying bottles against the light is to suspend them by wires, either from hooks or from bottoms of shelves. Care must be taken, though, that they are tied securely; otherwise anything from mishap to catastrophe can result.

In displaying bottles against light, a choice of harmonious colors is essential. As the light brings out the various hues, they mingle together visually in a shimmering dance. A clear bottle or two may be included in a tight grouping in order to provide "breathing space" in which the colors may fuse.

Although shelf display is probably the most satisfactory answer for many collectors, individual bottles of special beauty or interest, such as the cobalt blues or amethysts, or some of the rich olive or light greens, may be used to brighten and enhance the atmosphere of the home itself.

Approach the challenge with flare. There is no limit to the number of pleasing arrangements or combinations one can achieve.

The mantelpiece is an ideal setting, if your nerves can take watching the family cat stroll around it. Table tops and shadow boxes also provide niches for brilliant displays. A window seat or bay window will give you an inspired setting for artistic expression. Here, from sunrise to sunset, the play of light around your bottles may be unequaled anywhere else in the house.

To paraphrase a geometric axiom, in order to create a pleasing whole, the sum of its parts must blend and unify. Bottle shapes and colors should be carefully considered and chosen for small displays. One must simply keep adding, subtracting, arranging, and rearranging until one is completely content with the result.

If you have no artistic training, remember the hen and her chicks—one big shape partly surrounded by several smaller ones. Watch out for distracting elements, such as bottles that are too bright in hue, or a shape that stands out too sharply from the other in a group.

Depending upon the desired size of the display, and also depending on what the arranger is trying to say, one to five bottles should generally be enough.

Small groupings also need a base, such as a straw place mat or small rug. Any textured or nappy material, such as burlap or wool, gives heavy bottles a firm base. Velvet or cloth (perhaps a silk scarf or some leftover curtain material) help lay a pleasing ground for small bottles.

Use other available materials too, such as flowers, dried berries, porcelain figures, leaves, driftwood, pebbles, etc.

Other small displays might feature only one bottle: for instance, a historical flask enhanced by a piece of bunting, a newspaper clipping, campaign button, or model car of the period. Displays of this type are effectively housed in their own individual glass cabinets, or placed among other such displays.

The main thing is to let your imagination and innate esthetic sense come to the fore. For both art's and practicality's sake, however, strive for simplicity. Remember that whatever the display—unless it is encased in a cabinet—it is going to collect grime and dust very quickly, so it shouldn't be so elaborate that it can't be taken apart and cleaned regularly.

Glass, to be beautiful, should sparkle.

CHAPTER XVII

Forming a Bottle Club

Along with your own private bottle hunting down country lanes or in city alleys, you will find ways of augmenting your collection with quality items from antique shops and other collectors.

Once you know what to look for in a bottle, you will be able to judge what price is reasonable and which is not.

Browsing in antique shops along the highway is fun. It can also be profitable if you know what to look for. It can be disastrous if you don't.

When an antique dealer offers you a certain Beam bottle for, say, $50, you'll know whether it is a fair market price; another may be worth only $10. If you are offered an original Booz bottle, it will be a good thing if you are able to identify it from the hundreds of reproductions that have been made.

One way of increasing your bottle knowledge is by reading everything on the subject. Libraries offer a variety of fine books written by antiques experts and well-known bottle collectors.

Another sure way of increasing your know-how is by joining or forming a bottle club.

Bottle collectors are just like any other group of fans; they enjoy getting together and talking about their favorite subject.

If you know of a bottle club already in existence, and not too far away to attend meetings regularly, try for membership. There are sure to be a few bottle experts, eager to impart whatever they know, in a club already established.

If there is an antique dealer nearby he should be able to direct you to such a group.

You can, of course, form your own club if no other is available. Even three or four members, meeting regularly and pooling knowledge and experiences, can accomplish a great deal and bring another dimension to your collecting.

A bottle club, in bringing interesting people together, performs several important functions. Take bottle-hunting trips, for instance.

Tramping in the woods by oneself or with the wife and kids is fun, but after you get to a certain stage in this hobby, the urge often comes to share more broadly.

Whether it's a hiking party or a dune-buggy safari, joining with others and their families as they embark on a mass hunt is an exciting adventure.

Up at the first show of light in the sky, the steaks and hot dogs are packed, the Thermos bottles filled. A gobbled breakfast and a hasty cup of coffee while a hurried phone call is made to another member just to make sure he is awake. A dash about the house making sure nothing's been forgotten.

Don't forget the boots. Don't forget the map. Don't forget the paper towels. Don't forget the mustard. Don't forget your good humor.

As the first bits of sun come up over the horizon, you are on your way. Soon you will meet the others, bubbling over, as you are, with the excitement, and whether your day takes you to an Indian mound in New England or a ghost town in Colorado, you will come back to your house tired, refreshed, and the proud possessor of some more crusty gems to add to the shelf.

What nicer way to spend a day? Searching for buried treasure, breaking for a hearty lunch of sizzling steaks and roasted corn, and imbibing the joys of being in the out-of-doors with good companions. Captain Kidd's private crew never had it so good.

Other important benefits of belonging to a bottle club include the opportunities to see the collections of fellow members.

Along with informative inspection of bottles and general discussion groups, planned exhibits may be scheduled, with members competing for prizes. Here you will learn how best to display your bottles so that they will give you pleasure and allow you to easily identify them when showing them to others.

Trading is usually brisk at bottle-club meetings, and even the novice collector will augment his modest collection with items he would not otherwise be able to obtain. So always put away some duplicates for this purpose.

A couple of times a year, the club might bring in an expert—an antique dealer or collector—to discuss his own bottles, comment on the exhibits of members, and help with identifying bottles.

Perhaps the club may be able to rent a little space somewhere for a modest, but selective, library. If that isn't possible, members may chip in to subscribe to publications or books to be sent round-robin style.

Some bottle clubs actually put out a newsletter for their members. These can be brightly written minutes of meetings, notices of special exhibits, interviews with bottle experts, reviews of new books, swap columns, and chatty personal items.

A newsletter can be lots of fun, although it usually means a lot of hard work, too, for someone. But if dealers and antique-shop owners can be persuaded to advertise, it can be a source of income for the club, enabling it to broaden its scope of activity even further.

So do look at the bottle club as a pleasant and educational extension of your own individual activities—and join up!

You'll be glad you did.

Glossary of Terms

Applied Lip. Mouth of the bottle formed after being separated from the blowpipe.

Applied Ring Top. On bottles made after 1790, neck rings were applied after the bottles were taken from the blowpipe. Sometimes this was one ring, sometimes more. A layer of glass was made and put around the neck of the bottle.

Automatic Bottle Machine. This device, in which the entire bottle was produced, was invented in 1903.

Batch. Mixture of raw materials that is placed in a furnace to be melted into glass.

Bitters. So-called medicinal liquids of high alcoholic content that were mixed with various herbal ingredients. Also the bottles that held these liquids, often marked in glass.

Black Glass. Some of the earliest bottle glass whose impurities made it such a dark green as to appear black.

Blister. Bubble or other imperfection in glass.

Blob Top. The round, rather heavy lip that was common to mineral-water containers.

Blow Mold. A mold into which glass is blown to be shaped.

Blowpipe. A long hollow iron rod which is dipped into hot glass. The "gather" is then blown into, to produce a rounded shape.

Booz Bottle. A very well-known bottle in log-cabin shape, made for a Philadelphia distiller by the name of E. G. Booz.

Carboy. A large glass container for whiskey, often wicker-covered. This early bottle normally held about five gallons, but some held as many as ten.

Charge. Batch. The mixture of raw ingredients which is fed into the furnace to be melted into glass.

Chestnut. These small, round-shaped flasks, holding about half a pint, were among the first made in America. Often called Pitkin Chestnut.

Color In. The addition of metallic oxides, such as iron, cobalt, and chromes to color glass.

Commemorative. Pictorial flask honoring some national event.

Cullet. Parts of broken bottles used to form part of a new batch.

Cut Glass. Glass decorated by grinding, cutting, and polishing.

Decanter. Any of a wide variety of fancy bottles used for serving whiskey, gin, or wine. Bottles of special design in which liquor is packaged for holiday giving.

Demijohn. Having the round, long-necked shape of the carboy, but smaller, holding about four gallons.

Dunmore. Early globular wine bottle of the eighteenth and early nineteenth centuries, similar to the Hogarth bottle.

Embossing. Stamped-in-glass lettering describing the contents or the manufacturer. Only about 10 per cent of all bottles were stamped.

Figural. A bottle which has been molded into the shape of a person, animal, or common object.

Flint. The English first introduced this brilliant glass made with lead. The name comes from the fact that it was first made with powdered flint.

Free-Blown. This refers to bottles made without the use of a mold. Consequently, there are no mold seams on the bottles, and the shapes are often irregular.

Gather. When the blowpipe is dipped into hot glass, the blob that is pulled out is called the "gather." This is then blown to form a rounded shape.

Gaffer. Head glass blower, foreman of a glass handshop.

Grenade. A bottle "ball," filled with liquid, and used for putting out small fires.

Hogarth. Eighteenth-century spirits bottle so-called because it is shown in engravings of Hogarth's "Rake's Progress."

Historical Flask. Bottle commemorating some historical personage or event.

Kick-Up. Indentation caused by pushing bottom end of bottle up into bottle, usually one to two inches. A kick-up gives a bottle extra strength, especially needed in champagne bottles.

Leather Jack. A bottle for liquor made from leather.

Metal. After the raw materials are fed into the furnace, and the batch is melted, this molten mass is called "metal."

Mold. A hollow wooden, metal, or clay form consisting of two or more sections into which hot glass is dropped to shape a bottle.

Mold-Blown. Shaped by blowing within a mold.

Mold Mark. A seam made by the mold where it joins together.

Pattern-Molded. After having first been blown into a mold, the bottle is redipped or further blown to "expand" the original design.

Piece Mold. Several sections make up a piece mold: base, neck, and lip.

Pressed Glass. Glass which is made by "pressing" molten glass into a mold.

Pictorial Flask. Relief design on bottle showing some scene or object.

Pitkin. Small chestnut-shaped flask with design of ribbing or swirled ribbing.

Pontil. Also called punty rod, this iron rod was coated with hot glass on one end and used to take a blown bottle from the blowpipe. When it was broken off, it left a pontil mark or scar.

Pontil Mark. Scar on bottom of bottle left by pontil rod. These marks were often quite jagged and rough, and are one means of identifying older bottles.

Punt. Hot lozenge or blob of glass that was applied to the shoulder of a free-blown bottle. Sometimes the name of the owner of the bottle, or the year of its vintage was impressed into the lozenge before it cooled. Seal bottles were often called "punts" (*see* Seal below).

Quilting. Cross-hatched or diamond-shaped design.

Seal. Early spirits bottle upon which punts or blobs of hot glass were applied, and on which was stamped the vintage year and often the name of the person to whom the bottle belonged as well.

Sheared Top. Sheared tops appeared largely on early American bottles, those quite rough in shape. When the glass was still hot, the bottleneck was cut with a pair of shears. These sheared tops left sharp edges, and had no other lip. Rings were applied just below the top of these sheared edges.

Whittle Marks. Cold molds or lack of ideal temperatures often caused irregularities such as pits or bubbles in glass. Sometimes these marks were caused by roughness in a mold being used for the first time.

51 APPLIED LIP
CR: *Old Sturbridge Village*

52 APPLIED RING TOP
CR: *Old Sturbridge Village*

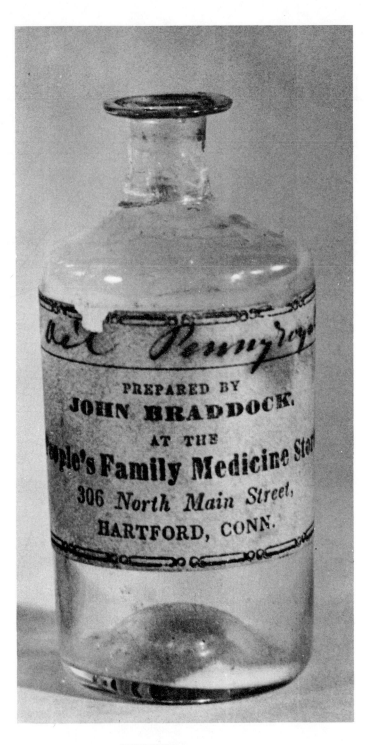

PREPARED BY
JOHN BRADDOCK,
AT THE
People's Family Medicine Store
306 North Main Street,
HARTFORD, CONN.

53 BITTERS
CR: *Old Sturbridge Village*

54 BLISTERS

CR: *Old Sturbridge Village*

55 BLOB TOP
CR: *Old Sturbridge Village*

56 BOOZ BOTTLE
CR: *The Corning Museum of Glass*

57 CARBOY
CR: *The Corning Museum of Glass*

58 CHESTNUT
CR: *The Corning Museum of Glass*

59 COMMEMORATIVE
CR: *James B. Beam Distilling Company*

60 DECANTER
CR: *The Toledo Museum of Art*

61 DEMIJOHN

CR: *Old Sturbridge Village*

62 DUNMORE
CR: *The Corning Museum of Glass*

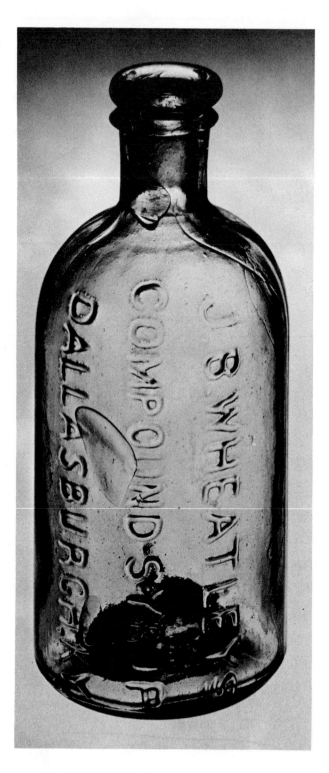

63 EMBOSSING
CR: *The Corning Museum of Glass*

64 FIGURAL

cr: *James B. Beam Distilling Company*

65 FREE-BLOWN
CR: *Old Sturbridge Village*

66 HISTORICAL FLASK
CR: *The Corning Museum of Glass*

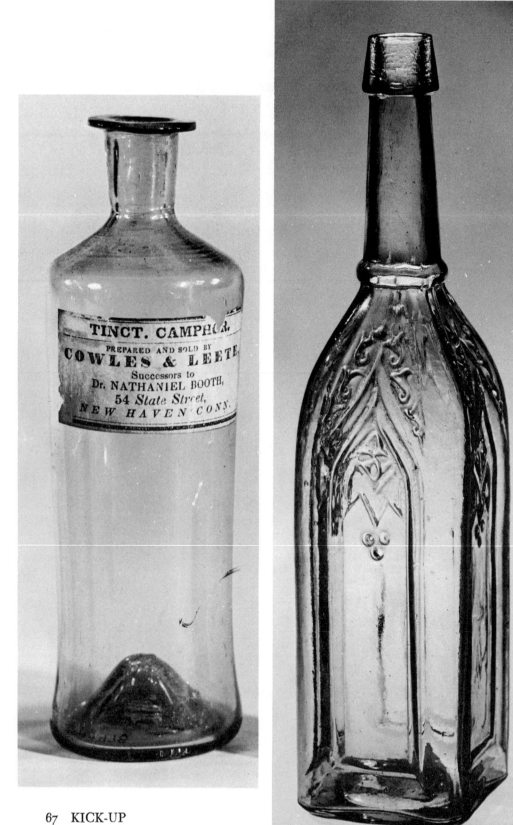

67 KICK-UP
CR: *Old Sturbridge Village*

68 MOLD-BLOWN
CR: *The Corning Museum of Gla*

69   MOLD MARK
CR: *The Corning Museum of Glass*

70 PIECE MOLD
CR: *Old Sturbridge Village*

71 PICTORIAL FLASK
CR: *The Corning Museum of Glass*

72 PITKIN
CR: *The Corning Museum of Glass*

73 PONTIL MARK
CR: *The Corning Museum of Glass*

74 QUILTING
CR: *The Corning Museum of Glass*

75 SEAL
CR: *The Corning Museum of Glass*

76 SHEARED TOP
CR: *The Corning Museum of Glass*

77 WHITTLE MARKS
CR: *Old Sturbridge Village*

INDEX

Look Inside a
Tree

Richard Spilsbury

Heinemann
LIBRARY

Chicago, Illinois

© 2013 Heinemann Library
an imprint of Capstone Global Library, LLC
Chicago, Illinois

Edited by Rebecca Rissman, Dan Nunn, and John-Paul Wilkins
Designed by Steve Mead
Original illustrations © Capstone Global Library Ltd 2013
Illustrations by Gary Hanna
Picture research by Ruth Blair
Production by Alison Parsons
Originated by Capstone Global Library Ltd
Printed in China

16 15 14 13 12
10 9 8 7 6 5 4 3 2 1

Library of Congress Cataloging-in-Publication Data
Spilsbury, Richard, 1963-
  Tree / Richard Spilsbury.
    p. cm.—(Look inside)
  Includes bibliographical references and index.
  ISBN 978-1-4329-7198-4 (hb)—ISBN 978-1-4329-7205-9 (pb)
  1. Trees—Microbiology--Juvenile literature. 2. Microorganisms—Juvenile literature. 3. Niche (Ecology)—Juvenile literature. I. Title.

QK475.8.S75 2013
582.16—dc23

2012011822

Acknowledgments
We would like to thank the following for permission to reproduce photographs: iStockphoto pp. 24 (© Martin Pot), 25 (© Michael Pettigrew), 27 (© DAMIAN KUZDAK); Naturepl pp. 9 (© Andrew Cooper), 19 (© Ingo Arndt), 26 right (© Andy Rouse); Shutterstock pp. 5 left (© Bruce MacQueen), 5 right (© Marek CECH), 6 (© Gorilla), 7 (© lafoto), 8 (© Virunja), 11 (© D. Kucharski & K. Kucharska), 12 (© jack53), 13 (© mlorenz), 14 (© FloridaStock), 15 (© Erik Mandre), 17 (© alslutsky), 18 (© Sergey Toronto), 20 (© Mark Bridger), 21 (© peresanz), 23 (© fotosav), 26 left (© visceralimage), 28, 29 (© Smit).

Cover photograph of a may-bug grub (*Melolontha vulgaris*) reproduced with permission of Shutterstock (© fotosav).

We would like to thank Michael Bright and Diana Bentley for their invaluable help in the preparation of this book.

Every effort has been made to contact copyright holders of any material reproduced in this book. Any omissions will be rectified in subsequent printings if notice is given to the publisher.

Disclaimer
All the Internet addresses (URLs) given in this book were valid at the time of going to press. However, due to the dynamic nature of the Internet, some addresses may have changed, or sites may have changed or ceased to exist since publication. While the author and publisher regret any inconvenience this may cause readers, no responsibility for any such changes can be accepted by either the author or the publisher.

Contents

Some words are shown in bold, **like this**. You can find out what they mean by looking in the glossary.

Among the Branches

A tree is a **habitat**. It provides different animals with food and **shelter**. Some animals live and feed mostly among the branches of a tree.

Chickadees are small, busy birds that hop along branches looking for food. They eat **insects**, **caterpillars**, spiders, and berries. They make **nests** and lay eggs in holes in trees.

▲ There are many different kinds of chickadee.

A honeybee flies to a tree and walks along the branches. It sucks up sweet **nectar** from flowers. Its long tongue is hollow and works like a drinking straw!

▼ This honeybee is feeding on a tree flower.

▲ Honeybee swarms contain thousands of bees.

Swarms of honeybees sometimes make **nests** on tree branches. They use nectar to make honey in the nest. They store the honey to eat in winter, when there are not many flowers around.

7

The gray squirrel is a **mammal** that spends most of its life up trees. It uses its strong teeth to feed on nuts and seeds. The squirrel's long, bushy tail helps it to balance as it leaps from branch to branch.

Squirrels collect food from the branches. ▶

▲ Baby squirrels huddle together to stay warm.

Female squirrels make **nests** among the branches. Baby squirrels are safe and warm in a nest. They only come out to eat nuts after their teeth have grown.

In the Trunk

Some animals live for part of the time inside a tree **trunk**. Others search for animals to eat under the **bark** of trees.

Bark beetles bite through tree bark to eat the soft wood underneath. They also lay eggs under bark. **Larvae** that **hatch** from the eggs eat the wood, too.

▲ Bark beetles eat wood from tree trunks.

Barn owls make **nests** in holes in tree **trunks**. The **female** owl sits on the eggs to keep them warm until the babies **hatch**. The **male** owl catches and brings her food.

▼ This barn owl is peering out from its nest.

▲ Barn owls fly silently.

Barn owls eat mice, frogs, and other small animals. They sit and listen for **prey** scurrying on the ground. Then they swoop down to catch it.

Woodpeckers ▶
have heavy,
pointed beaks.

Woodpeckers
peck quickly to
make holes in tree
trunks. Then they make
their **nests** inside. Adult
birds will attack owls and
other birds that try to eat eggs
or chicks from their nest.

Woodpeckers grip tree trunks using their strong **talons**. They poke their sharp beaks under the **bark** to feel for **insects** to eat. Their long, sticky tongues pick up the insects they find.

This woodpecker is ▶ feeling for insects with its tongue.

Around the Base

Some smaller animals crawl up onto trees around the base. Other larger animals stand by trees and nibble at parts of the **trunk** they can reach.

Holly blue butterflies fly around trees. **Females** lay eggs on ivy that grows up tree trunks. Green **caterpillars** then **hatch** from the eggs and eat ivy buds, berries, and leaves.

▲ Holly blue butterflies have striped **antennae.**

A ladybug is a kind of beetle. Birds eat a lot of beetles, but they usually leave ladybugs alone. Ladybugs' bright colors warn birds that they taste bad!

▼ Red and black colors are a warning signal.

Some ladybugs ▶ huddle together in cracks in tree trunks when it gets cold.

Ladybugs crawl along tree **trunks** looking for small **insects** to eat. Many ladybugs sleep in gaps under the **bark** during winter, when it is too cold to find much food.

Some deer live in woodlands. They feed on buds, leaves, nuts, and berries. In the winter, deer sometimes eat the **bark** off trees, when other food is hard to find.

▼ These deer are alert to danger.

antlers

The antlers ▶
of male
deer can
grow very
large.

Young **males**
scratch their new
antlers against tree
trunks. This rubs off
the skin that protects
the antlers while
they grow. But it can
damage some trees.

21

Among the Roots

Many animals find **shelter** and food in the ground beneath a tree. They live in the soil and dead leaves among the **roots**.

Some beetles lay their eggs in the soil among tree roots. Curled, white **larvae hatch** from the eggs and eat the roots. They grow and change into beetles.

▲ Beetle larvae eat and eat so they can grow.

Many millipedes live among tree **roots**. They mostly come out at night to chomp dead leaves. Millipedes do not see well, so they feel their way along using their **antennae**.

▼ A millipede is on the move!

▲ Millipedes come in many different colors.

Millipedes are long, thin animals with many legs. All of their little legs move quickly to help them crawl through soil. When scared, millipedes curl up tight.

Badgers often dig large holes to live in beneath tree **roots**. The roots hold up the roofs of their **dens**. They stay in the dens in the day and come out at **dusk** to feed and play.

▼ The American badger (left) and European badger (right) are slightly different colors.

▲ Badgers are shy and try to avoid humans.

Badgers use their tough claws to dig out dens and food from the soil. They have wide, flat teeth to chew worms and **larvae**. They also eat frogs, slugs, and other small animals.

Tree Habitats

Spring and summer are the seasons when many trees have leaves and flowers. Many animals visit trees because there is lots of food to eat. Most baby animals are born at this time, too.

▼ This is a tree in summer.

▲ This is a tree in winter.

In the winter, many trees lose their leaves. The branches are bare and the ground is cold. Fewer animals visit trees, and some sleep underground in **nests** and **dens**, waiting for spring to come.

Glossary

antennae (singular: antenna) thin parts on the heads of some animals, including beetles and lobsters, that are used to feel and touch

antler bony body part that grows on a male deer's head

bark tough outer covering of a tree trunk and branches

caterpillar young stage in the life cycle of a butterfly or moth

den hidden home or resting place of some animals, such as badgers or bears

dusk time of day just before night

female sex of an animal or plant that is able to produce eggs or seeds. Males are the opposite sex.

habitat place where particular types of living things are likely to live. For example, polar bears live in snowy habitats and camels live in desert habitats.

hatch come out of an egg

insect type of small animal that has three body parts, six legs, and usually wings. Ants and dragonflies are types of insect.

larvae young of some animals, such as insects

male sex of an animal or plant that is unable to produce eggs or seeds. Females are the opposite sex.

mammal animal that has hair and feeds its babies with milk from the mother. Humans and squirrels are types of mammal.

nectar sweet liquid made by flowers to attract insects and other animals

nest place where a bird or other animal lays eggs or cares for its young. Nests are often made from twigs or grass.

prey animal that is caught and eaten by another animal

root underground part of a plant that takes in water and useful substances from the soil

shelter place that provides protection from danger or bad weather

swarm large group of flying insects

talon claw of a bird

trunk part of a tree above the ground that supports the tree's branches

Find Out More

Books

Cooper, Sharon Katz. *Rotten Logs and Forest Floors* (Horrible Habitats). Chicago: Raintree, 2010.

Kalman, Bobbie. *Baby Animals in Forest Habitats* (Habitats of Baby Animals). New York: Crabtree, 2011.

Llewellyn, Claire. *Forests* (Habitat Survival). Chicago: Raintree, 2013.

Web sites

Facthound offers a safe, fun way to find web sites related to this book. All of the sites on Facthound have been researched by our staff.

Here's all you do:

Visit www.facthound.com

Type in this code: 9781432971984

Index